The Socratic Individual

The Socratic Individual

*Philosophy, Faith, and Freedom
in a Democratic Age*

Ann Ward

LEXINGTON BOOKS
Lanham • Boulder • New York • London

Excerpt(s) from THE BIRTH OF TRAGEDY AND THE CASE OF WAGNER by Friedrich Nietzsche, translated by Walter Kaufmann, translation copyright © 1967 by Walter Kaufmann. Used by permission of Random House, an imprint and division of Penguin Random House LLC. All rights reserved.

Ann Ward. (forthcoming). "Poetry, Philosophy and Faith in Kierkegaard's Philosophical Fragments," in Writing the Poetic Soul of Philosophy: Essays in Honor of Michael Davis, Denise Schaeffer ed. St. Augustine's Press.

Reprinted from Ann Ward, "Abraham, Agnes and Socrates: Love and History in Kierkegaard's Fear and Trembling," in Love and Friendship: Rethinking Politics and Affection in Modern Times, Eduardo A. Velasquez, ed. (Lanham, MD: Lexington Books), 2003. All rights reserved

Published by Lexington Books
An imprint of The Rowman & Littlefield Publishing Group, Inc.
4501 Forbes Boulevard, Suite 200, Lanham, Maryland 20706
www.rowman.com

6 Tinworth Street, London SE11 5AL, United Kingdom

Copyright © 2020 by The Rowman & Littlefield Publishing Group, Inc.

British Library Cataloguing in Publication Information Available

Library of Congress Cataloging-in-Publication Data

Title: The socratic individual: philosophy, faith, and freedom in a democratic age / Ann Ward.
Description: Lanham : Lexington Books, 2020. | Includes bibliographical references and index. |
    Summary: "This book explores the recovery of Socratic philosophy in 19th century political
    thought of G.W.F. Hegel, Soren Kierkegaard, John Stuart Mill, and Friedrich Nietzsche. For
    Kierkegaard the Socratic individual in modern times is the person of faith, for Mill the idiosyncratic public intellectual, and for Nietzsche the Dionysian artist"-- Provided by publisher.
Identifiers: LCCN 2020001254 (print) | LCCN 2020001255 (ebook) | ISBN 9781793603777 (cloth) |
    ISBN 9781793603784 (ebook) | ISBN 9781793603791 (pbk)
Subjects: LCSH: Philosophy, Modern--19th century. | Political science--Philosophy. | Socrates.
Classification: LCC B803 .W28 2020 (print) | LCC B803 (ebook) | DDC 190.9/034--dc23
LC record available at https://lccn.loc.gov/2020001254
LC ebook record available at https://lccn.loc.gov/2020001255

For Mary

Contents

Acknowledgments

I wish to acknowledge my friend and teacher Mary Nichols. It was as a graduate student in her class at Fordham University on the role of heroism in nineteenth-century political thought that the ideas for this book first took root. I also wish to thank Mary Nichols, as well as my colleagues David Nichols and David Clinton, for encouraging and making possible my becoming a member of the graduate faculty at Baylor University. My gratitude is also owed to my editor at Lexington Books, Joseph Parry, for his support of my research, and to the anonymous reviewers of my manuscript whose insightful comments and my attempts to address them have made this a better book.

Parts of chapter 1 appear as "Socrates, Democracy, and the End of History," *The European Legacy: Toward New Paradigms* (forthcoming) 2020. An extended version of chapter 2 was originally published as "Abraham, Agnes, and Socrates: Love and History in Kierkegaard's *Fear and Trembling*," in *Love and Friendship: Rethinking Politics and Affection in Modern Times*, Eduardo A. Velasquez, ed. (Lanham, MD: Lexington Books, 2003, 297–337). Parts of chapter 3 appeared as "Socratic Irony and Platonic Ideas? Kierkegaard's 'Critique' of Socrates in *The Concept of Irony*," in *Socrates: Reason or Unreason as the Foundation of European Identity*, Ann Ward, ed. (Newcastle, UK: Cambridge Scholars Publishing, 2007, 164–77) and "Poetry, Philosophy and Faith in Kierkegaard's *Philosophical Fragments*," in *Writing the Poetic Soul of Philosophy: Essays in Honor of Michael Davis*, Denise Schaeffer ed. (St. Augustine's Press, 2019, 155–76). An earlier version of chapter 5 originally appeared as "Art and the Voice of the Cosmos in Nietzsche's *Birth of Tragedy*," in *Socrates and Dionysus: Philosophy and Art in Dialogue*, Ann Ward, ed. (Newcastle, UK: Cambridge Scholars Publishing, 2013, 124–37). I would like to thank the publishers, editors and anonymous reviewers of these collections and journals for their thoughtful reading and support of my work.

I wish to acknowledge Lee Ward, my husband and colleague, for his love and friendship throughout the writing of this book and our long career together as both students and academics. Finally, I wish to thank my daughter Mary. She has let me see the beauty and independence of an individual soul as it strives to grow and touch something higher.

Ann Ward
Baylor University
September 2019

Introduction

The Recovery of Socrates in Nineteenth-Century Political Thought

One of the primary legacies of Leo Strauss's life work is the revival of the study of classical political philosophy, especially that of Plato's Socrates (Pangle, 2006: 43).[1] Having become submersed in the study of the classics, Strauss's students today are characterized by their approach to the history of political philosophy as a debate between ancients and moderns, Socratic rationalism versus Enlightenment principles. Strauss's turn to Socrates, however, is a manifestation of a philosophic movement that began in earnest in the nineteenth century. This book will explore the recovery and revival of Socratic philosophy in nineteenth-century political thought, particularly the thought of G. W. F. Hegel, Soren Kierkegaard, John Stuart Mill, and Friedrich Nietzsche. I will investigate the cause of the renewed interest in Socrates in these nineteenth-century thinkers, the particular way in which each one of them understood and thus transformed Socratic philosophy in their works, and the "costs," as it were, as well the benefits of reviving Socrates in our current age.

The cause, I argue, of the revival of interest in the person of Socrates and his philosophic way of life can be found in Hegel's assertion in the "Introduction" to *The Philosophy of History* that, "the State is the Divine Idea as it exists on Earth" (*PH* 39).[2] The divine in the modern state, representing the completion of the historical process, is to be found in its laws. Thus, in deifying the state, Hegel deifies the rationally apprehended moral or ethical rules that inhere between the citizens of the state. The individual, therefore, at the end of history takes the state as their end, becoming one with the whole which is the state by assenting to and obeying the laws of the state. In accepting and obeying such rational laws, the individual ceases to be solely a feeling being and becomes a thinking being, ruled by reason rather than

1

passion. In the process they acquire not only freedom and morality, but divinity as well. At the end of history man becomes God in the state, by becoming a thinker rather than a lover, and humanity as such becomes completely revealed or known. Can Socratic philosophy, which questions the laws and authoritative opinions of the political community on behalf of gods or ideas that are higher than it, continue once the modern liberal state emerges at the end of history? For Hegel, it seems there can be no appeal to something beyond modern law and politics to critique such modern law and politics; in the modern state we have reached the perfection of humanity and history. Socratic skepticism, therefore, should cease when the modern state comes into being.

Hegel's call for the absorption of the individual within the modern, liberal state and the concomitant claim that Socratic skepticism should cease because history has reached its end and perfection, I argue, is the cause of the attempt to recover and revive the pursuit of Socratic philosophy in the nineteenth century. Recoiling from Hegel's attempt to chain the individual within the "cave," as it were, nineteenth-century thinkers push back against Hegel's deification of the state (*Rep* 514a–515c).[3] Yet, in contrast to classical liberalism, nineteenth-century thinkers do not hold up the rights-bearing individual against the claims of society and the state. Classically liberal philosophers such as John Locke argued that in the state of nature human individuals are equal and bear certain natural rights, most importantly the rights to life, liberty and property that exist prior to and can never be understood to be laid down for the sake of political society. Indeed, rights-bearing individuals bring political society, or the state, into being for the sole purpose of protecting these rights, understood as ends to which the state is subordinated. Hegel, however, rejects the liberal understanding of the rights-bearing individual and its notion of the state. Hegel argues that the state of nature populated by individuals with natural rights never existed in history, and if it did, the individuals described by liberal philosophy in this state are bodily beings without rational capacity and hence see the state as a limit to their freedom rather than its realization (*PH* 40–41). For Hegel, however, the state does not limit human freedom but rather makes it possible, allowing individuals, through absorption into the political whole, to become rational beings rather than merely feeling or material beings.

Underlying Kierkegaard, Mill and Nietzsche's turn to or at least interest in Socrates, I suggest, is their acceptance of Hegel's critique of the liberal conception of the rights-bearing individual. Like Hegel, they appear to agree that such an individual is an unworthy competitor to the state and hence unable to counter the collectivizing tendencies of the historicist movement that Hegel inaugurated. In search of a worthy individual to hold up against the state and counter the belief in the "end" of history, Kierkegaard, Mill and Nietzsche bring Socrates back from antiquity and into the future, as it were.

The Socratic philosopher in modern times, therefore, can provide an example of the beauty of individuality against the totalizing attempts of the modern state, in a way that the liberal individual cannot. Yet, I argue that there is a cost to such a project. In the Platonic dialogues we discover a Socrates who tries to live his life according to reason (*logos*), going wherever the better argument takes him. In the *Republic* in particular, Socrates and his interlocutors construct in speech a just soul in which reason rules spiritedness, and reason together with the help of spiritedness rules the desires. The ancient Socrates, in other words, is a rational Socrates. In the philosophies of Kierkegaard, Mill, and Nietzsche, however, Socrates has undergone a significant transformation. All three nineteenth-century philosophers portray the soul of Socrates as subordinating reason to passion; passion is understood as the core of and highest part of the Socratic philosophers' soul. The beauty of individuality in our democratic age, therefore, for these thinkers seems to come at the price of a darker foundation in irrationality.

I begin my investigation of the nineteenth-century return to Socrates by considering, in chapter 1, Hegel's claim in the "Introduction" to his *Philosophy of History* that Socrates advanced beyond Anaxagoras by attempting to connect universal reason to concrete human particulars by means of his theory of ideas or forms. In doing so, according to Hegel, Socrates turns from the study of material nature to the rational human soul as it is drawn to the good. In addition, Socrates believed that provided one philosophized, one could grasp the ideas in any place at any time. Hegel himself, however, must advance beyond Socrates because the latter failed to understand that the universal manifested itself slowly in successive stages in the historical process, only becoming fully actualized at the end of history. Philosophy, therefore, or the mind's access to truth is only possible in modernity. Moreover, universal reason takes concrete form, according to Hegel, in the modern liberal state, and the individual, having their end in this state, achieves their highest potential by obeying and thereby internalizing the state's laws.

For Hegel, I argue, Socratic philosophy, which questions the laws and authoritative opinions of the political community on behalf of gods or ideas that are higher or independent of it, having no grounds in liberal modernity must come to an end. Yet, when we turn to analyzing Hegel's suggestion near the end of the "Introduction" that Socrates is a philosophic World-historical individual—a type of individual who undermines their society to bring forth a new order—we can see that Hegel nonetheless considers Socrates as possessing greatness. Socrates undermines his society through his questioning that leads to the ideas, the latter creating a split between the ideal and reality of a people. Once this split emerges, it is problematic for political society in two ways: first, discussion of the ideas undermines the doing of the virtues in favor of speaking and thinking about them, and second, the particular manifestations of the virtues never live up to their universal ideals, thereby encouraging its members to see their society as defective.

In chapter 2 I explore Søren Kierkegaard's response in *Fear and Trembling* to Hegel's deification of the state at the "end of history." Through his pseudonym "Johannes de Silentio" or "John of Silence," Kierkegaard argues that if Hegel is right and we in liberal modernity have achieved the highest so that humanity has been perfected and history has come to an end, then there is nothing left for us to do. Human greatness disappears because all difficult but beautiful tasks to inspire noble youths have ceased. What does Kierkegaard suggest these tasks are? In contrast to Hegel's deification of reason, Kierkegaard believes the human essence is passion and hence the highest task is to love. Kierkegaard thus seeks to remind us modern liberal democrats of what it means to love, providing models of human greatness who pursued this noble task. For Kierkegaard the greatest love is the love of God. Abraham, therefore, as the father of faith, is the foremost model of human greatness that Kierkegaard presents in *Fear and Trembling*. However, since very few individuals in any generation can experience the faith of Abraham, Kierkegaard puts forward other forms of love which are analogous to but differ from faith. The most important of these is Socratic philosophy. Moreover, I argue that as Kierkegaard's work concludes, we discover that *Fear and Trembling*, which began as eulogy to Abraham and the life of faith, is actually a eulogy to Socrates and the life of philosophy.

Kierkegaard, therefore, in contrast to Hegel who argues for its end, presents Socratic philosophy as crucial for human flourishing in liberal modernity. Moreover, Kierkegaard presents the greatness of Socrates and that of Abraham as attained by transcending and even violating the rational moral order of one's political community. Kierkegaard thus pushes back against Hegel's call for the absorption of the individual into the state at what the latter believes is the end of history. Rather, in presenting Abraham and Socrates as models of human greatness for noble individuals in liberal modernity to emulate, Kierkegaard encourages such individuals to transcend the modern state and the bounds of their time, and possibly even reason itself, thereby ensuring that history and human greatness do not disappear.

In the first part of chapter 3 I explore Kierkegaard's *Concept of Irony*. In the "Introduction" to this work, Kierkegaard claims that irony was the substance of Socrates' life. Socratic irony in this sense was more than simply a speech act in which Socrates said the opposite of what he meant, but it was also a way of living. Kierkegaard indicates the full import of Socrates' ironic way of life by characterizing irony as a negative process through which Socrates posited his subjectivity or individual identity against the moral and intellectual norms of his age. By means of his irony, therefore, Kierkegaard argues as Hegel does that Socrates destroyed Greek society. Yet, according to Kierkegaard, Socrates is destructive of his society not because he posits universal ideas above the particulars to which the latter can never live up to, as Hegel maintains. Rather, Kierkegaard suggests that Socrates' assertion of his subjectivity, although displacing the old, fails to offer a positive alternative to the established order, the imperfections of which being revealed collapses.

I further my investigation of Kierkegaard's restoration of the true meaning of Socratic irony by exploring the question of what, for Kierkegaard, belongs to Socrates and what belongs to Plato in the Platonic dialogues. I conclude that whereas Socrates asks the questions, Plato provides the answers, the ideas or forms. Moreover, I suggest that in his attempt to disentangle Socrates from Plato, Kierkegaard brings to light an image of Socrates as more than just an individual asserting his subjectivity against the external world, but as the embodiment and object of an *eros* that draws human beings toward a higher individuality rather than the universality of the Ideas or Forms.

In the second part of chapter three I turn to an analysis of Kierkeagaard's *Philosophical Fragments*. In this work, under the pseudonymous authorship of Johannes Climacus, Kierkegaard initially explores the relationship between philosophy and faith by contrasting Socrates and the god as teachers. Socratic questioning, Kierkegaard argues, causes the recollection of truths that were already in the learner. Learning is thus re-affirmation of the self and discarding of the teacher. The god, on the other hand, is a savior who brings knowledge of truth that was beyond the learner. Learning is the discarding of self as one accepts what only the god can give

Despite this initial contrast between Socrates and the god as teachers, I argue that Socratic philosophy and religious faith in *Fragments* are both brought together as well as drawn apart. Kierkegaard first attempts to bring philosophy and faith together by giving a rational account of why an important tenet of Christianity, that the god becomes human, seems necessary. The most significant way, however, in which Kierkegaard brings philosophy and faith together is through his understanding of the condition necessary for grasping the truth brought by the god. This condition involves becoming aware of our ignorance, an awareness that is also brought about by the type of Socratic dialectic described in Plato's *Apology of Socrates*. Yet, Kierkegaard's understanding of philosophy and faith also diverge. For instance, Christianity's beginning point in the existence of god, Kierkegaard suggests, is not open to rational demonstration but rather presupposes faith.

When drawing philosophy and faith, and hence Socrates and the god, apart, Kierkegaard puts forward an image of Socrates that the *Concept of Irony* would regard as a "Platonic" Socrates. This Socrates, as in the *Meno*, asks "speculative" questions designed to turn the learner inward to recollect ideas or universal truths within themselves that were there but had been forgotten. In this image the philosophic teacher is dispensable and can be cast off as soon as the truth is grasped. Yet, when Kierkegaard begins to draw philosophy and faith, Socrates and the god, together, he puts forward an image of Socrates that the *Concept of Irony* would regard as the ironic or truly "Socratic" Socrates, as it were. This Socrates, as in the *Apology of Socrates*, asks questions not designed to bring forth answers or lead the learner to universal truths within themselves, but rather to show the learner that there are no stable truths human reason grasp. In this way the "Socratic" Socrates, like Abraham, always keeps the "unknown" as a passionate particularity beyond the universal in front of him, aware that in his search for this passionate or erotic unknown, he is ultimately searching for an unknown part of himself.

Like Kierkegaard, John Stuart Mill, to whose thought in *On Liberty* I turn in chapter 4, is far from thinking as Hegel does that Socratic philosophy is unnecessary and even unhelpful to the freedom that emerges in liberal modernity. On the contrary, Mill, like Kierkegaard, suggests that it is precisely the Socratic questioning of authoritative opinions that brings into doubt the supposedly rational moral order of one's society, that ensures the flourishing of human freedom in the modern liberal, democratic order.

Mill indicates, therefore, that his understanding of the freedom possible in his time is very different from Hegel's understanding of freedom. For Hegel, freedom means overcoming the individuating constraints of the body and its passions by obeying and thereby internalizing the rational laws of the modern state. In so doing a person becomes one with the whole and free to think rather than simply feel. Mill, on the other hand, argues that his main concern for the future is to protect and foster the development of individuality in the face of a social tyranny more formidable than many kinds of political oppression. Damaging to the soul of the person, social tyranny enforces conformity to society's ideas and practices in a way that prevents any individual exceptionalism or idiosyncrasy from arising.

The type of liberty Mill is thus interested in is almost the opposite of that which Hegel envisions; for Mill it is the freedom of each to construct their own unique, individual identity without fear of moral coercion or the social stigma that can result when we differ from our fellow citizens, provided we do no harm to others in the process. Thus, whereas Hegel argues that the individual has the state as their end, Mill believes freedom, in Socratic fashion, is defining oneself against it. Moreover, the individuality that liberal freedom makes possible arises, according to Mill, from the erotic "desires" and "impulses" at the core of the soul, the energy from which, properly sublimated, accounts for any intellectual energy the individual may have. Thus, like Kierkegaard, Mill locates human greatness, as it were, not in a universal reason that makes human beings the same, but rather in the passions that make us different and set some unique but indispensable individuals at odds with the reigning social and moral order of their time. Yet, despite these similarities with Kierkegaard, Mill differs from the latter in suggesting a strong distinction between Socratic dialectic that makes possible diversity in thought and lifestyle, and faith. Indeed, Mill is quite critical of religious belief, and Christianity in particular, in a way that Kierkegaard is not.

Mill's critique of Christianity brings him into agreement with philosopher Friedrich Nietzsche, to whose thought I turn in chapters 5 and 6. In *The Birth of Tragedy*, Nietzsche accuses Christianity of a hatred for passion, beauty, and sensuality that is hostile to life itself. To counter Christianity's will to death, as it were, Nietzsche invokes the Greek god Dionysus, apparently calling for a renewal of paganism in our time. Moreover, Mill's fear that the equality of democracy poses serious dangers to individual exceptionalism is also shared by Nietzsche. In *Beyond Good and Evil*, Nietzsche argues that the egalitarian morality of democracy brands the highest and strongest drives, those which ground the excellence and superiority of exceptional individuals, as pathological, therefore seeking to suppress all true human greatness and virtue in the world.

Despite these agreements, however, Mill and Nietzsche diverge in their attitudes toward Socrates. Whereas Mill celebrates Socratic philosophy as that which can ground the space for individual diversity in the face of the tyranny of public opinion and the conformity it seeks to impose, Nietzsche attacks Socratic philosophy as one of the key problems. Like Christianity, Socratic rationalism, according to Nietzsche, is at war with the older, Dionysian craving for the ugly, animal nature of human beings manifested in their bodily passions and desires. Moreover, far from being a resource against the leveling tendencies of democracy, in "The Problem of Socrates" Nietzsche argues that Socratic dialectic is only possible with the coming of democratic equality. With respect to the intellectual energy of the select few, whereas Mill argues that this requires the liberal freedom to think and act as you please provided you do not harm others, Nietzsche believes precisely the opposite. In direct contrast to Mill, Nietzsche argues that human excellence requires the imposition of strict moral rules that are obeyed over a long period of time.

In their embrace of Socrates and Socratic philosophy, both Kierkegaard and Mill express a concept of an exceptional individual the core or height of whose soul is not reason but passion. In *The Birth of Tragedy*, although not embracing Socrates, Nietzsche does seek to displace the authority of reason, not simply for the sake of the passions but, going further, to explore the body itself and its sexual longing for fusion with the unintelligible mass of matter that it senses living behind the intelligible universe. Thus, coming full circle, whereas Hegel conceived of freedom as overcoming the individuating constraints of the body and living as pure mind, Nietzsche seeks to get exceptional human beings back in touch with their bodies and hence their sexual natures. To do so one has to reject the Socratic rationalism which seeks to master the body and its longings and return to the Dionysian. Yet, when

Nietzsche concludes *Beyond Good and Evil* with the invocation of Dionysus, he presents this god, I argue, as practicing a Socratic dialectic that makes us aware of our ignorance. Thus, just as we discover that Kierkegaard's eulogy to Abraham turns into a eulogy to Socrates, perhaps Nietzsche's call to revive Dionysus is in fact a call to revive a Socratic form of philosophy.

Although there is a wealth of scholarship on the political thought of G.W.F. Hegel, Soren Kierkegaard, John Stuart Mill, and Friedrich Nietzsche, there are few books that focus on the role of Socrates in the works of each of these nineteenth-century philosophers. One exception is *Socrates in the Nineteenth and Twentieth Centuries*, edited by Michael Trapp. The essays in this collection argue, as I do, that philosophers such as Kierkegaard and Nietzsche are in dialogue with Hegel when they write about Socrates and acknowledge that Socrates goes through a radical transformation when recovered by these philosophers.[4] Moreover, in his piece on Hegel, Glenn Most argues that Hegel viewed Socratic dialectic as ultimately destructive of the Greek culture that it questioned.[5] Yet, in contrast to Most who investigates the understanding of Socrates in Hegel's *History of Philosophy*, I explore the significance of Socratic philosophy for Hegel in his *Philosophy of History*. Moreover, although Most accurately identifies the significance of the Socratic turn for Hegel as that which directs the Western intellectual tradition away from the physical world to the psychic world of thought thinking itself, I go beyond Most in arguing that for Hegel the universality of human reason can only be grasped at the end of history and so necessarily eluded Socrates.[6] Once full knowledge has been achieved at the completion of history, Socratic philosophy, like history, comes to an end.

Two books similar to this one are Catherine's Zuckert's *Postmodern Plato's* and Dana Villa's *Socratic Citizenship*. In *Postmodern Plato's*, Catherine Zuckert explores the return to Platonic philosophy, and hence to Plato's Socrates, to discover the original character of philosophy in the West and thus the roots of their own activity, in the philosophies of Friedrich Nietzsche, Martin Heidegger, Hans-Georg Gadamer, Leo Strauss and Jacques Derrida.[7] Although it lacks an analysis of the importance of Plato's Socrates to the philosophies of Søren Kierkegaard and John Stuart Mill, there are a number of similarities between the argument in *Postmodern Plato's* and the one presented here. As I do, Zuckert argues that the revival of interest in Plato for these nineteenth- and twentieth-century thinkers stemmed directly or indirectly from Hegel's claim that, having developed a real science that could explain all, he had brought philosophy as the search for wisdom to an end.[8] Not persuaded by Hegel's claim, Nietzsche and Heidegger engaged in a series of unconventional rereadings of Plato. Yet, similar to my argument that Nietzsche eulogizes Socrates indirectly through his eulogy to Dionysus, the god of tragedy, both Nietzsche and Heidegger, according to Zuckert, conclude from their studies that as philosophy as it had been practiced in the

West is no longer possible we must therefore turn to "poetry" in its place.[9] In response to Nietzsche and Heidegger, Gadamer, Strauss and Derrida engage in their own rereadings of Plato. Whereas Gadamer concludes that philosophy does not have an end, Strauss concedes that philosophy may indeed end but that this is not necessary or fated; for Derrida philosophers cannot answer the question of philosophy's possible end.[10]

Another area of agreement between Zuckert's argument and my own is the post-Hegelian stance toward early modern thought. As I argue that Kierkegaard, Mill and Nietzsche turn to Socrates as an exemplar of the beauty of individuality because they accept Hegel's premise that the rights-bearing individual of classical liberalism is unworthy to posit against the state, Zuckert argues that the thinkers she explores are "postmodern" due to their conviction that, "modern rationalism has exhausted its promise and possibilities."[11] Desirous of creating something new beyond modernity, these postmodern thinkers are not primarily interested in what Plato meant to his contemporaries as to what he can mean for future generations. Moreover, similar to my argument that in disentangling Plato from Socrates Kierkegaard calls into question the truth of the "ideas," Zuckert argues that all five postmodern thinkers she addresses question the truth of Plato's "doctrine" of ideas, coming to believe that Platonic philosophy was not a set of arguments or doctrines, but rather a way of life.

Dana Villa's *Socratic Citizenship,* while also lacking an analysis of Kierkegaard's thought on Socrates, does explore the role of the Socratic model in the political thought of Mill, Nietzsche, Max Weber, Hannah Arendt and Strauss, with Mill's depiction of Socrates being the most important. Although there are many similarities between the argument of this book and that of Villa's *Socratic Citizenship*, there are three significant ways in which Villa offers an alternative interpretation of the meaning of Socrates and the recovery of his thought in the nineteenth century. First, Villa argues that Plato's *Apology of Socrates* shows that Socrates was the inventor of "moral individualism" in the West.[12] Socrates' moral individualism takes the form of asserting what Villa characterizes as a "dissolvent rationality" against the conventional moral norms of the state, in which Socrates exercises a "ruthless intellectual honesty" in his refusal to obey authority to avoid doing anything unjust.[13] Socrates, therefore, makes possible the notion of a "conscientious, moderately alienated citizenship," if not fully articulating a philosophy of full-fledged civil disobedience.[14]

The argument of this book differs in the sense that it understands the Socrates of Plato's *Apology* as engaged in the search for truth, something which Villa denies.[15] The concept of Socrates as engaged in the search for individuality against the collectivizing attempts of the state is an innovation, I argue, of nineteenth-century thought, arising out of its acceptance of Hegel's critique of the liberal, rights-bearing individual. A more significant way, however, in which Villa's interpretation of the impact of Socrates' "moral individualism" on nineteenth-century thought diverges from my own is Villa's understanding of Socrates' questioning of authoritative opinions as an example his "secular conscience."[16] By "secular conscience" Villa means that Socrates does not question the customary laws and authoritative opinions of the state on the basis of his understanding of truths beyond or higher than the state, such as "natural law," "the voice of god," or even it seems the ideas. Rather, he does so on the basis of his "self-agreement," meaning that Socrates is concerned that he not contradict himself in presenting his principled arguments for avoiding injustice; Socrates is concerned that he make logically consistent arguments for disobeying state authority.[17]

The problem, I believe, with this interpretation of the "secular conscience" is that it actually points to the absorption of the individual, including Socrates, in the Hegelian state at the end of history. This becomes especially apparent in Villa's critique of Sophocles' Antigone. Villa argues that Antigone cannot be properly viewed as having a conscience, let alone a "secular conscience," and thus cannot serve as a model of moral individualism or even civil disobedience, because her resistance to Creon, "deeply conservative in character," is grounded in traditional religious and family duties that take priority over the values of the state.[18] Thus, although Villa turns to Socrates as a model of civil disobedience flowing from individual judgment of the law and state authority, he rejects any invocation, such as made by Antigone, of principles outside of or above the law and state authority to justify the critique of such authority. In other words, it appears that Villa is advocating something like state-approved "civil disobedience." This would take the form of such things as state sanctioning and funding of secular civil society groups and state-led education in secular, liberal values.[19]

That Villa's argument for secularism actually points to moral absorption within the Hegelian liberal state is related to the second significant way in which the argument in *Socratic Citizenship* differs from my own. Villa argues as I do that Mill's defense of the near absolute freedom of speech in chapter 2 of *On Liberty* is, in effect, "his attempt to translate the chief virtues of Socratic dialectic into a form appropriate to modern society."[20] Moreover, one of the main virtues of Socratic dialectics and hence a "moral individualism" in modernity, Villa concedes, is that in contesting all received truths, it prevents the consolidation of opinion that advances along with advances in modern scientific knowledge. However, Villa proceeds to argue that Mill does not defend Socratic dialectics and individuality because he values pluralism or diversity of opinion for its own sake. Rather, according to Villa, Mill believes Socratic dialectics will lead to "moral progress" whose "teleology" is a "consensus on the most important issues."[21] What is "moral progress" for Mill which requires "consensus"? According to Villa, "[f]or Mill there was no contradiction between increased liberty, tolerance, and

diversity of opinion, on the one hand, and the increasingly universal acceptance of the fundamental moral theses of rights-based individualism, on the
other. [. . .] Fostering [. . .] an openness to an indefinite number of paths to
the 'good life' did not mean for Mill [. . .] that we must affirm traditional
religious or communal forms of life."[22] Curiously, therefore, Villa argues
that Mill believes secular liberal opinion regarding rights should be shielded
from the "dissolvent rationality" of Socratic dialectic, while at the same time
the latter is used in Hegelian fashion to suppress traditional religious and
cultural modes of thinking and acting.

The third significant way in which *Socratic Citizenship* provides an alternative interpretation to my own is its denial of any substantial discontinuities
between the political philosophy of Mill and that of Nietzsche. For instance,
although Villa argues that both Mill and Nietzsche were opponents of a
"dogmatic" Christianity, he does not acknowledge that for Nietzsche, in
contrast to Mill, Christianity is simply one more manifestation of the democratic movement whose origins he traces to Socrates.[23] More importantly but
briefly, is that Villa portrays Nietzsche's "sovereign individual" who rejects
"obedience to authority" as almost identical to the moral individual of Mill's
thought, who exercises a Socratic dialectic in modernity, and to the Socrates
of "secular conscience" in Plato's thought, who seeks agreement with himself or logical consistency in opposing received moral conventions.[24] Not
only does this differ significantly from my argument that for Nietzsche, in
contrast to Mill, human excellence requires the imposition of and engage-
ment with strict moral codes obeyed over a long period of time, but it also
implies, once again, that the telos for Nietzsche's "secular," "sovereign"
individual is actually absorption within the liberal, Hegelian state. It is to
Hegel's argument for the deification of the state and the end of Socratic
philosophy that we shall now turn.

NOTES

1. Thomas L. Pangle, *Leo Strauss: An Introduction to His Thought and Intellectual Legacy* (Baltimore: Johns Hopkins University Press) 2006.

2. G.W.F. Hegel, *The Philosophy of History*, J. Siberee trans. (New York: Dover Publications), 1956. All subsequent citations will be taken from this edition.

3. See Plato, *Republic*, Allan Bloom trans., (New York: Basic Books) 1968. All subsequent
citations will be taken from this edition.

4. Michael Trapp, "Introduction: the nineteenth-and twentieth-century Socrates," in *Socrates in the Nineteenth and Twentieth Centuries*, M.B. Trapp ed., (Aldershot, UK: Ashgate
Publishing, 2007), xviii; and Glenn W. Most, "Socrates in Hegel," in *Socrates in the Nineteenth
and Twentieth Centuries*, M.B. Trapp ed., (Aldershot, UK: Ashgate Publishing, 2007), 3.

5. Most, "Socrates in Hegel," 8.

6. Ibid., pp. 5–6.

7. Catherine Zuckert, *Postmodern Platos: Nietzsche, Heidegger, Gadamer, Strauss, Derrida* (Chicago: University of Chicago Press, 1996): 1.

8. Zuckert, *Postmodern Platos*, 2.

9. Ibid., 4, 7.
10. Ibid., 7.
11. Ibid., 1.
12. Dana Villa, *Socratic Citizenship* (Princeton: Princeton University Press, 2001): 1.
13. Ibid., 3, 5, 27.
14. Ibid., 2.
15. Ibid., 80–81.
16. Ibid., 15.
17. Ibid., 40–41.
18. Ibid., 51–52.
19. Ibid., 52, 107. Also, see Villa's approval of Mill's proposals in *Representative Government* for such measures as plural voting to allow the state to give minority voices legislative representation and real power against the wishes of the majority. Villa, *Socratic Citizenship*, 111–14.
20. Ibid., 75.
21. Ibid., 89.
22. Ibid., 91.
23. See Villa, *Socratic Citizenship*, 132.
24. Ibid., 125, 133–35, 150–53.

Chapter One

Socrates, Democracy, and the End of History

The Socratic Turn in Hegel's Philosophy of History

In the introduction to his *Philosophy of History*, Hegel initially argues that Socrates advanced beyond Anaxagoras, attempting to connect universal reason to concrete human particulars by means of his theory of ideas or forms. In doing so, Socrates turns from the study of material nature to the rational human soul as it is drawn to the good. In addition, Socrates believed that provided one philosophized, one could grasp the ideas in any place at any time. Hegel himself, however, must advance beyond Socrates because the latter failed to understand that the universal manifested itself slowly in successive stages in the historical process, only becoming fully actualized at the end of history. Philosophy, therefore, or the mind's access to truth is only possible in modernity. Moreover, universal reason takes concrete form, according to Hegel, in the modern liberal state, and the individual, having their end in this state, achieves their highest potential by obeying and thereby internalizing the state's laws.

For Hegel, I argue, Socratic philosophy, which questions the laws and authoritative opinions of the political community on behalf of gods or ideas that are higher or independent of it, having no grounds in liberal modernity must come to an end. Yet, when we turn to analyzing Hegel's suggestion near the end of the "Introduction" that Socrates is a philosophic World-historical individual—a type of individual who undermines their society to bring forth a new order—we can see that Hegel nonetheless considers Socrates as possessing greatness. Socrates undermines his society through his questioning that leads to the ideas, the latter creating a split between the ideal and reality of a people. Once this split emerges, it is problematic for political society in two ways: first, discussion of the ideas undermines the doing of the virtues in favor of speaking and thinking about them, and second, the particular manifestations of virtue never live up to their universal ideals, thereby encouraging its members to see their society as defective.

Herbert Marcuse, atypical of Hegel scholars, provides a brief analysis of the importance of the Socratic turn to Hegel's conception of the role of thought in the process of history. Marcuse recognizes that for Hegel Socrates reoriented philosophy away from the Anaxagorean focus on material nature to the study of "subjectivity," or what I term the rational human soul seeking to discover the good, understanding, "that this Right and Good is in its nature universal."[1] Moreover, turning to "subjectivity," Socrates, Marcuse argues, discovered the ideas or the "essence[s] of things as distinguished from their appearance."[2] Socratic philosophy thereby allows persons to comprehend that "[t]here are beautiful things in the state, good and brave deeds, true judgements, just judges—but something exists that is the beautiful, the good, the brave [. . .]; it is more than all these particulars and common to all of them. Man has an idea of the beautiful, the good [. . .] in his *notion* of beauty, goodness. [. . .]"[3] The significance of the Socratic turn, therefore, for Hegel's concept of history according to Marcuse, is that "[p]hilosophy began to elaborate universal concepts [. . .] Universal concepts, however, are abstract concepts, and 'the construction of the State in the abstract' struck at the very foundation of the existing state."[4] Marcuse thus argues, as I do, that Hegel, conceiving of Socrates as a type of philosophical World-historical individual, "connected the destructive dynamics of thought with *historical* progress toward 'universality'."[5] Thought is destructive, moreover, because setting "the truth apart as a universal and attribute[ing] the knowledge of this universal to the autonomous thought of the individual," it produces a split between the ideal and the reality of the state that encourages its citizens to see the latter as defective.

Despite Marcuse's insights into the importance of the Socratic turn to Hegel's conception of history, he does not seem to recognize, as I do, that for Hegel the coming together of the universal and the particular, the ideal and the real, in the modern liberal state, means that the Socratic form of philosophy, like history, should and does cease. Marcuse's limitation in this regard is connected to his contention that Hegel's thesis, "Reason is the sovereign of the world," does not actually imply "that history has a definite end."[6] Although he acknowledges that it seems to be the case for Hegel that freedom is perfected in the liberal, bourgeois state, Marcuse argues that the historical laws of progress, "to ever higher forms of freedom, [. . .] cease to operate if man fails to recognize and execute it. [. . .] Progress depends on man's ability to grasp the universal interest of reason and on his will and vigor in making it a reality."[7] Marcuse, therefore, seems to imply that if persons do not have "self-consciousness of freedom" in the modern, liberal democratic state, they are free to practice a Socratic form of philosophy to overturn it while remaining within the Hegelian worldview.[8]

SOCRATES AND ANAXAGORAS

In the "Introduction" to his *Philosophy of History*, Hegel makes direct or indirect reference to Socrates three times: first, in the latter's relation to and improvement upon the doctrine of Anaxagoras, second, as an exemplar of the Greek spirit, and third, near the end of the "Introduction," as a type of philosophical world-historical individual. We will begin with Socrates' relation to Anaxagoras.

Hegel's argument in the "Introduction" that both humanity and history reach their completion in the modern liberal state arises in the context of his treatment of "Universal History" (*PH* 1). The subjects of Universal History, according to Hegel, are not individual human beings but rather "Peoples" or "Totalities that are States" (*PH* 14). Hegel contends that the investigation of these phenomena of Universal History by philosophic historians such as himself, gives rise to the thesis that "Reason governs the World" (*PH* 9, 11, 14). This is the same as saying that "God governs the World," and thus that the history of the world is a rational or divine process (*PH* 9, 13, 15, 36). Reason, like God, is the "Infinite" or the universal, and as the universal, it, like the philosophic historian himself, is not concerned in its governance of the world with particular human beings, but rather with the political communities in which they exist (*PH* 14). There is no particular Providence but, as God himself is the universal, only a general providence. Moreover, Reason, like God, is the "absolutely powerful essence," and thus is responsible for all being and becoming in the universe, which includes both the natural and the human worlds, or "both physical and psychical nature" (*PH* 9, 16). Thus, just as God in His governance of the world, "can . . . will nothing other than himself," the aim of Reason is to "reveal itself in the World," and thus to make itself manifest or actualized in concrete form both in nature and in history (*PH* 9–10).

This is not the first time that we have encountered the thesis that reason governs the world. As Hegel aptly points out, "the Greek Anaxagoras was the first to enunciate the doctrine that *nous*, Understanding generally, or Reason, governs the world" (*PH* 11, 269). Arguing that "Socrates adopted the doctrine from Anaxagoras, and it forthwith became the ruling idea in Philosophy," Hegel proceeds to give a brief commentary on Socrates' account, recorded in Plato's *Phaedo*, of his encounter and ultimate disappointment with Anaxagoras' teachings (*PH* 12). Turning to the *Phaedo*, we discover Socrates disillusioned with pre-Socratic natural science in his search for the causes of birth, growth, decay and then death in material nature, but then telling his interlocutors, "I heard someone reading from a book he said was by Anaxagoras and said that it is in fact Mind that puts the world in order and is responsible for all things" (*Phaedo*, 97c).[9] Thinking that he had finally found, "a teacher after [his] own mind, a teacher concerning the cause of the things that *are*," Socrates believes that Anaxagoras will demonstrate that:

> Mind [. . .] in ordering the world, would order all things and position each thing in just the way in which it is best. So if somebody should want to discover the cause concerning each thing—in what way it comes into being or perishes or *is*—he'd have to discover this concerning it: in what way it's best for it to be or undergo or do anything whatsoever. Now by this account, it benefits a human being, in this matter and in all others, to look to nothing but what's most excellent and best (*Phaedo*, 97c–d).

Socrates' assumption on first hearing that mind or reason orders, or is the cause of, the world, is that Anaxagoras, as the above passage makes clear, will explain why it is good or best that things in the world are what they are or do what they do. The desire for such an explanation reflects what can be called Socrates' "teleology"; understanding things in terms of their final cause, or their highest purpose or perfection. Yet, Socrates is soon disappointed. Absorbed in reading the books of Anaxagoras, Socrates eventually, "saw a man who didn't employ mind at all and didn't hold any causes responsible for putting things in order, but instead put the blame on air and ether and water and other things many and absurd" (*Phaedo* 98c, also see *PH* 12). Anaxagoras, in other words, is a materialist, describing not why but how things do what they do according to universal and hence rational laws of material nature. Thus, in trying to explain why he would remain in prison and await the death sentence imposed on him by the Athenians rather than flee, Socrates speculates that Anaxagoras:

> After saying that Socrates does everything he does by mind and then venturing to assign the causes of each of the things I do—should first say that I'm now sitting here because my body's composed of bones and sinews, and because bones are solid and have joints keeping them separate from one another, while sinews are such as to tense and relax and also wrap the bones all along with the flesh and skin that holds them together. Then since the bones swing in their sockets, the sinews, by relaxing and tensing, make me able, I suppose, to bend my limbs right now—and it's through this cause that I'm sitting here with my legs bent (*Phaedo* 98c–d).

Anaxagoras, Socrates suggests, can say how he sits in prison—because he has joints that can bend and sinews that are flexible—but not why it is good or best that he sit in prison and await death. Hegel indicates his agreement with Socrates' assessment of Anaxagoras when he says of the latter's understanding of the thesis that reason governs the world, "it is not intelligence as self-conscious reason—not a Spirit as such that is meant [. . .] The movement of the solar system takes place according to unchangeable laws. These [universal] laws are Reason, implicit in the phenomena in question. But neither the sun nor the planets, which revolve around it according to these laws, can be said to have any consciousness of them" (*PH* 11). For Hegel, as for Socrates, although there may be universal, rational laws that govern matter in motion, matter does not have rational participation in or consciousness of these laws. Thus, the reason that Anaxagoras refers to is not the reason that Hegel or Socrates have in mind. Socrates indicates his understanding of reason as cause when, in an alternative explanation to why he sits in prison awaiting death, he says:

> Since the Athenians judged it better to condemn me, so I for my part have judged it better to sit here and more just to stay put and endure whatever penalty they order. Since [. . .] these sinews and bones of mine would, I think, long ago have been in Megara or Boeotia, swept off by an opinion about what's best, if I didn't think it more just and more beautiful, rather than fleeing and playing the runaway, to endure whatever penalty the city should order (*Phaedo* 98e–99a).

Socrates thus points to the human soul and the human mind within it, or more specifically his soul and his mind, directed or drawn toward the good, as that which governs his body and determines his actions. Socrates' rational soul determines his actions and makes him who he is, a rational soul apparently absent in Anaxagoras' thought. As a result of his disappointment with Anaxagoras' abstraction from the rational human soul, Socrates embarks on what he calls a "second sailing in search of cause" (*Phaedo* 99d). Socrates' "second sailing" is in effect a turn away from the direct investigation of material nature, or from pre-Socratic natural science, to the investigation of the human soul moved by the good (also see *PH* 269). Yet, Socrates says that he could not look at either the physical beings, the soul, or the good directly but only indirectly, and so, according to Socrates, "it seemed to me that I should take refuge in accounts and look in them for the truth of the beings" (*Phaedo* 99e). Taking refuge is speeches, Socrates discovers what he calls "those much-babbled-about things," the ideas or forms, such as the "Beautiful Itself by Itself and a Good and a Big and all the others" (*Phaedo* 100b).

Hegel makes reference to Socrates' theory of ideas or forms as an advance upon the thought of Anaxagoras, when he says:

> The ignorance of Anaxagoras, as to how intelligence reveals itself in actual existence, was ingenuous. Neither in his consciousness, nor in that of Greece at large, had the thought been farther expanded. He had not attained the power to apply his general principle to the concrete, so as to deduce the latter from

the former. It was Socrates who took the first step in comprehending the union of the Concrete with the Universal (*PH* 13).

Anaxagoras, therefore, did not apply the universal, or the rational laws of nature, to the concrete things of human beings. Unable to apply his understanding of reason to the particular human phenomena, Anaxagoras' thought was confined to the realm of material nature—how things do what they do—as opposed to human nature—questioning why things do what they do and hence focusing on the rational human soul. Anaxagoras, therefore, could not comprehend the historical, or the progressive movement of history. According to Hegel:

> The changes that take place in [material] Nature—how infinitely manifold so ever they may be—exhibit only a perpetually self-repeating cycle; in Nature there happens "nothing new under the sun," and the multiform play of its phenomena so far induces a feeling of *ennui*; only in those changes that take place in the region of Spirit does anything new arise. This peculiarity in the world of mind has indicated in the case of man an altogether different destiny from that of merely natural objects—in which we find always one and the same stable character, to which all change reverts;—namely, a *real* capacity for change, and that for the better—an impulse to *perfectibility* (*PH* 54).

Socrates, unlike Anaxagoras, attempted to connect the universal with the particular, or tried to think about the human things in a universal and hence rational way. Socrates thus moved beyond the realm of material nature and made the rational human soul drawn toward the good the center of his philosophy. Socrates did this, Hegel indicates, through his theory of ideas or forms. How do the ideas or forms allow for this? Taking the Idea of the Beautiful as an example, Socrates claims that all of the particular manifestations of beauty, such as "a blossoming color or shape" or a beautiful human deed, are beautiful "because [they] participate in that Beautiful" (*Phaedo* 100c, d). Socrates continues and says, "nothing makes a thing beautiful but the presence of or communion with that Beautiful," and, "it's by the Beautiful that all beautiful things are beautiful" (*Phaedo* 100d, e). Socrates appears to suggest that the idea of the Beautiful is that universal or common characteristic which all particular examples of beauty participate in or share; it is that quality or "class characteristic" of beauty that makes the beautiful things what they are—beautiful—and thus what allows us to speak of them as beautiful.

In his discussion of the philosophic quest near the beginning of the *Phaedo*, Socrates indicates that whereas the particular manifestations of the ideas in the material, sensible world, such as a beautiful color, shape or deed, can be grasped by the senses of the body, the ideas themselves, such as the Beautiful Itself, can only be grasped by reason in the soul. Socrates thus suggests that the ideas, while in the sensible world inasmuch as they move through and hence make the particulars what they are, also transcend the sensible world at the same time (*Phaedo* 65e–66a). The ideas therefore, aim to connect particular human actions and perceptions in time to thought about the universal, or to beauty itself and the good itself. If Socrates, as Hegel argues, comprehended "the union of the Concrete with the Universal," and hence thought about the rational human soul drawn toward the beautiful and the good, or to the *perfect*, why is Socratic philosophy incomplete? Why does Hegel, in other words, have to move beyond Socrates? We will return to this question below.

SPIRIT IN WORLD HISTORY

Returning to Hegel's thesis that reason governs the world, in it he collapses Reason with God, the rational with the divine. The term which he gives to both Reason and God in their governance of the human as opposed to the natural world is "Spirit" (*PH* 10). The nature of Spirit, according to Hegel, has a number of abstract characteristics. Primarily, Spirit is "man as such" (*PH* 18). Thus, Spirit is that universal or common characteristic that all human beings share, uniting them into a class or species of being which distinguishes them not from each other, but from other classes or species of nonhuman beings. This universal characteristic is the capacity for reason or thought. The human is essentially a thinking or rational being. According to Hegel, "Thought is indeed essential. It is that which distinguishes us from the brutes" (*PH* 9). Moreover, "Thought contemplates everything in the form of Universality" (*PH* 438). Thus, to be fully human, Hegel indicates that the thinking mind must apprehend universal principles, such as the thinking mind itself; thought is that universal characteristic which all human beings share.[10] In other words, the fundamental fact of human equality or sameness in reason must be affirmed. Thus, Hegel claims that in thought, "the individual comprehends itself as person, that is, recognizes itself in its single existence as possessing universality—as capable of abstraction from, and of surrendering all speciality; and, therefore, as inherently infinite" (*PH* 70).

In order to understand what it means for the thinking subject to shed speciality for universality, and therefore to become a "man as such," Hegel claims that we can look to Spirit's direct opposite, "Matter" (*PH* 17). According to Hegel, Matter "is essentially composite; consisting of parts that exclude each other" (*PH* 17). Matter, as opposed to Spirit, individuates human beings from each other, the body and the passions derived from it concealing their common humanity, or their sameness in reason, from them. Individuation is an exterior or material phenomenon, rather than an interior one of the soul. Yet, according to Hegel, Matter "seeks its Unity; and therefore exhibits itself as self-destructive, as verging towards its opposite" (*PH* 17). Hegel therefore indicates that Matter has its end in Spirit, that individuals have their end in the universal. Thus, the highest task of the individual is to be ruled by the mind rather than the body, by reason rather than passion. Being so ruled, individuals transform themselves from feeling beings into thinking beings, thereby becoming conscious of that universal characteristic—Spirit or thought itself—which they share in common with all other human individuals. Their common humanity, or "man as such," is revealed to them. Hegel calls this consciousness of a common humanity—that all human beings are equally capable of thought and therefore of grasping universal principles—the "consciousness of Freedom" (*PH* 19). Individuals become aware that as rational or spiritual beings, human beings can be free from the individuating constraints of Matter. Thus, another characteristic which Hegel assigns to Spirit, that universal characteristic which all human beings share, is freedom: "we may affirm that the substance, the essence of Spirit is Freedom" (*PH* 17).

Spirit itself, according to Hegel, is that which brings about this consciousness of freedom or consciousness of itself, because Spirit has itself and nothing higher as its end (*PH* 19). Thus, Spirit's aim is that it "reveals itself in the world," and thus that it become or make itself manifest in concrete form on earth (*PH* 10). Yet, Spirit reveals or actualizes itself in time, or unfolds its nature through different and successive stages in the world's history. In these different stages, however, Spirit only becomes partially manifest, the full manifestation of Spirit only coming in the final stage, at which time the historical process comes to an end. At the completion of the world's history, according to Hegel, Spirit manages, "to make itself actually that which it is potentially," and thus to work itself out of its hiddenness and become completely disclosed (*PH* 17).

SOCRATIC PHILOSOPHY AND THE GREEK SPIRIT

Hegel argues that there are three major stages or epochs in the world's history, which correspond to three different but increasing levels of the consciousness of freedom or of Spirit itself. It is in this discussion of the stages of world history that Hegel makes his second (indirect) reference to Socrates. According to Hegel, in the "Oriental" world, in the past as well as the present, there is no knowledge that "Spirit-Man as such—is free" (*PH* 18, 104). Rather, they believe that only "one is free," the Despot (*PH* 18). Yet, the freedom of the Despot turns out to be his unrestrained indulgence in and imposition of his capricious will. His rule is characterized by "ferocity— (the) brutal recklessness of passion" (*PH* 18). Thus, it turns out that not even the Despot is free; all are governed by their passions, rather than by reason.

Humanity as such is completely concealed and all are reduced to the status of brutes. All are slaves, none are citizens. The second stage of world history is the Greek and Roman worlds. In this stage, Hegel argues that the Greeks and Romans, "knew only that some are free—not man as such. Even Plato [Plato's Socrates] and Aristotle did not know this. The Greeks, therefore, had slaves" (*PH* 18). Thus, in contrast to the Orient, where humanity is completely concealed, in Greece and Rome humanity becomes partially revealed. Some are thought capable of being ruled by reason, or of rationally comprehending universal principles, and thus are recognized as human, whereas some are thought to be ruled solely by the body and its passions, and thus are assigned to the status of brutes. In the Greek and Roman worlds there were two broad castes, the rational and the irrational, which allowed some to be citizens but caused others to be slaves. It seems that for Hegel, therefore, Socrates, although making the rational human soul the center of his philosophy, did not fully recognize that all human beings have a rational human soul or a soul capable of being governed by reason, and thus had an inadequate grasp of Spirit.

The third and final stage, and thus the completion of history, are the German nations. They were the first, according to Hegel, "to attain the consciousness, that man, as man, is free: that is the freedom of Spirit which constitutes its essence" (*PH* 18).[11] Thus, in the German nations, the fundamental fact of human equality in reason is completely revealed. All individuals come to be alike, and one cannot think of oneself without thinking of humanity at the same time; each individual represents the whole, because all are recognized as rational or equally capable of suppressing their particular passions and comprehending and adopting universal principles. Spirit, or reason—that universal characteristic which all human beings share— achieves its aim and becomes completely manifest, and all are allowed to be citizens, none are slaves.

The implications of this view of the stages of world history is that for Hegel all thought is relative to time or bound by the historical epoch in which one lives.[12] The historicity of thought, as it were, means that in the first two stages of world history the human mind does not have full access to Spirit, or the truth of the human equality in reason, and thus it does not in essence have full access to itself. Only at the end of time, in Hegel's time, a very special time in which the human becomes completely known, does the mind of the thinker have full access to truth.

The consequences to Socratic philosophy of Hegel's view of history are stark. Socrates, Hegel argues, moves beyond Anaxagoras in attempting to understand the particulars and the human things in terms of their universality, through his theory of ideas or forms. In doing so, Socrates turns from study of material nature to human nature, or the rational human soul drawn to the universal, and ultimately to the universal good. Yet, Socrates believed, mistakenly Hegel implies, that the universal or the ideas are above time, place, culture or the mind thinking about them. In other words, the human mind can have access to universal truth at any time anywhere provided one practiced Socratic philosophy or came into contact with a Socratic teacher. Socrates, therefore, although improving upon Anaxagoras turns out to be just as unhistorical as the latter. In abstracting from history and connected to Hegel's charge that he did not know that all human beings were capable of being ruled by reason, Socrates, like Anaxagoras, either cannot or will not recognize the inherent perfectibility of humanity as such at the end of history.

Hegel, on the other hand, believes that truth only comes to be in time, and is only fully manifested at the end of time when humanity and history have reached their perfection, and history thus comes to an end. The human mind, in other words, can only be fully connected with the universal, or contemplate the thinking mind itself, in Hegel's time. Philosophy, therefore, or the mind's access to universal truth, is only possible in modernity, and we and Hegel are necessarily more knowledgeable than Socrates. Moreover, not only is Socratic philosophy mistaken in its self-understanding, not connecting with the universal or the good as it believes, but, as we will see in the next section, it, like history, must come to an end when the modern state emerges.

THE STATE

At the end of history the concrete form which Spirit—the universal, rational, and divine—takes on earth is the modern state.[13] According to Hegel, "The (modern) state is the Divine Idea as it exists on Earth" (*PH* 39). The divine in the modern state is to be found particularly in its laws. Its laws are the embodiment of reason, first, because they are universal, applying equally to all, and second, because they recognize and ensure the equality and therefore freedom of all. For instance, they secure "Freedom of Property and Freedom of Person," as well as equality of opportunity in both economics and politics, to all members of the state (*PH* 447–48).[14] The modern state, for Hegel, although formally a constitutional monarchy, is clearly liberal bourgeois in character (*PH* 46, 104). Moreover, the rational laws of the modern state are also the laws of morality, according to Hegel. Thus, in deifying the state, Hegel deifies the rationally apprehended moral or ethical rules that inhere between the citizens of the state.

The individual at the end of history takes the state as his end. He sheds his particularity for universality, or becomes one with the whole which is the state, by assenting to and obeying, because they are rational, the laws of the state.[15] In accepting and obeying such rational laws, the individual adopts the universal or the general will as his own will, uniting or subordinating his private good to the common good (*PH* 38–39, 48). In doing so, the individual ceases to be solely a feeling being and becomes a thinking being, ruled by his mind rather than his body, or by reason rather than passion. In the process he acquires not only freedom and morality, but divinity as well. At the end of history man becomes God in the state, by becoming a thinker rather than a lover, and humanity as such becomes completely revealed or known. [16]

Can Socratic philosophy continue once the modern liberal state emerges at the end of history? As Plato illustrates in the *Phaedo* and many other of his dialogues, the Socratic way of life entails the individual's questioning of the laws and authoritative opinions of the political community on behalf of gods or ideas that are higher or independent of it. [17] Yet, in Hegel's conception, the universal, rational idea and the divine are not above the state but rather comprehended by it. Thus, for Hegel, it would seem that there can be no appeal to something beyond modern law and politics to critique such modern law and politics; in the modern state we have reached the perfection of humanity and history. Socratic skepticism, therefore, should cease when the modern state comes into being.

SOCRATES AS WORLD-HISTORICAL INDIVIDUAL

Hegel indicates that the actualization of Spirit in the modern state at the end of history also marks the proper end of the Socratic ideal. Yet, in his third (indirect) reference to Socrates near the end of his "Introduction," Hegel presents Socrates as a type of philosophical World-historical individual, and thus as someone possessing greatness and worthy of admiration. The concept of the World-historical individual is developed by Hegel when discussing the means that Spirit uses to achieve its end, the gradual unfolding of itself in successive stages in world history. The means Spirit uses are the particular, selfish passions of individuals, especially the selfish passions of those Hegel calls World-historical individuals. These latter persons, such as Alexander the Great, Julius Caesar and Napoleon Bonaparte, pursue their own private advantage, but in doing so unknowingly cause the next successive stage in the unfolding of history to occur; Spirit, or reason, works through their passions, as it were, to actualize itself in time (*PH* 31). [18] For instance, Hegel argues that Caesar's self-conscious motive for overthrowing the Roman republic and establishing himself as the "Autocrat" of the Roman state and gaining sovereignty over the entire Roman empire, was his fear of "losing a position [. . .] at least of equality with the others who were at the head of the State, and of succumbing to those who were just on the point of becoming his enemies" (*PH* 29). Yet the underlying cause, unknown to Caesar himself, for his actions was Spirit's intent to actualize the next successive stage in history and fuller manifestation of itself in time. According to Hegel:

The Autocracy of Rome—was [. . .] at the same time an independently necessary feature in the history of Rome and of the world. It was not, then, [Cae-
sar's] private gain merely, but an unconscious impulse that occasioned the
accomplishment of that for which the time was ripe. Such are all great historical men—whose own particular aims involve those large issues which are the
will of the World-Spirit (*PH* 30).

World-historical individuals, therefore, are not protectors of their own states
and societies, but are rather destroyers of them. Thus, unlike most persons
whose "course of action [. . .] is determined, as regards the ordinary contin-
gencies of private life, by the laws and customs of [their] State," World-
historical individuals, as "agents of the World-Spirit," are an exception; they
are betrayers of their State's laws and customs. Yet, this destructiveness of
World-historical individuals is intended by Spirit to achieve the next successive stage or unfolding of reason in history. For this reason, Hegel argues
that, "[t]hey may be called Heroes, inasmuch as they have derived their
purposes and their vocation, not from the calm, regular course of things,
sanctioned by the existing order; but from a concealed fount [. . .] from that
inner Spirit" (*PH* 30). Hegel lauds the greatness of these historical persons
despite their apparent cruelty and disdain for individual human life, claiming,
"[a] World-historical individual is devoted to the One Aim, regardless of all
else. It is even possible that such men may treat other great, even sacred
interests, inconsiderately; conduct which is indeed obnoxious to moral repre-
hension. But so mighty a form must trample down many an innocent flow-
er—crush to pieces many an object in its path" (*PH* 32). Hegel suggests that
the great ends of history, such as human equality and freedom in the modern
liberal state, justify any means, such as the brutality and destructiveness of
the World-historical individual.[19]

Hegel's initial examples of the great historical persons—Alexander the
Great, Julius Caesar and Napoleon Bonaparte—are all men of action and
great imperialists who destroyed their own states and historical epochs: Alexander destroyed the Greek *polis*, Caesar destroyed the Roman republic, and
Napoleon destroyed the European feudal order. Yet, in his third (indirect)
reference to Socrates, Hegel indicates that thought, and not just action, can be
destructive to the state and society in which it appears. The appearance of
philosophy in their midst, Hegel argues, causes a society to engage in a type
of collective self-reflection in which, "it is employed in rendering itself an
object of its own contemplation" (*PH* 76). The result is a split between the
reality of a society and the idealized version that its people have of it. Thus,
Hegel says of the result of philosophy's appearance:

We have then before us a *real* and an *ideal* existence of the Spirit of the
Nation. If we wish to gain the general idea and conception of what the Greeks
were, we find it in Sophocles and Aristophanes, in Thucydides and Plato

(Plato's Socrates). In these individuals the Greek spirit conceived and thought itself. This is a profounder kind of satisfaction which the Spirit of a people attains; but it is 'ideal,' and distinct from its 'real' activity" (*PH* 76).

Although Hegel names Sophocles, Aristophanes and Thucydides when speaking of how the Greek Spirit contemplated itself, he emphasizes that it is Socratic philosophy, by its focus on speech and discovery of the ideas, that carried this contemplation farthest and caused the most intense split between the reality and the idealized version of Greek society (also see *PH* 270). Thus, Hegel argues:

> At such time, therefore, we are sure to see a people finding satisfaction in the *idea* of virtue; putting *talk* about virtue partly side by side with actual virtue, but partly in the place of it [. . .] partly suggesting reasons for renouncing duties, partly itself *demanding reasons*, and the connection of such requirements with Universal Thought; and not finding that connection, seeking to impeach the authority of duty generally, as destitute of sound foundation" (*PH* 76).

Hegel indicates that in asking about the idea of virtue, Socrates is destructive of his society in two ways. First, he undermines the doing of the virtues in favor of thinking and speaking about them. Second, as the particular manifestations of the virtues in human society can never live up to the universal or ideal conceptions of them, Socrates encourages his interlocutors to think of their society and state in which these particular manifestations occur as defective; the ideal exists apart or above society and state.[20] From this, Hegel asserts, "the isolation of individuals from each other and from the Whole makes its appearance: their aggressive selfish and vanity; their seeking personal advantage and consulting this at the expense of the State at large" (*PH* 76–77). Socrates, therefore, is extremely destructive to his society; exposing the deficiency of the political community, selfish individualism and detachment from the whole breaks out.[21] He therefore seems to be a type of philosophical World-historical individual who lays the groundwork, as it were, for the political World-historical individual to emerge. Yet, if Spirit is fully actualized in the modern liberal state and history has thereby reached its end, World-historical individuals, intellectual or active, Hegel suggests, must and do disappear. If there are no more stages in World History requiring destruction of previous stages, then there is no more need for either philosophical or political greatness.

NOTES

1. Marcuse, *Reason and Revolution*, 243.
2. Ibid., 241.

3. Ibid., 243.

4. Ibid., 244.

5. Ibid., 240.

6. Ibid., 224–25; also see Allen Speight, *The Philosophy of Hegel* (Montreal & Kingston: McGill-Queen's University Press, 2008), 98; but see Findlay, *Hegel: A Re-Examination* (London: George Allen & Unwin Ltd., 1958), 322.

7. Marcuse, *Reason and Revolution*, 231.

8. Ibid., 231.

9. Plato, *Phaedo*, Eva Brann, et. al. trans. (Newburyport, MA: Focus Classical Library), 1998. All subsequent citations will be taken from this edition.

10. See Pierre Hassner. "Georg W.F. Hegel," Allan Bloom trans., in *History of Political Philosophy*, Leo Strauss and Joseph Cropsey eds. (Chicago: University of Chicago Press, 1987), 739.

11. See Joseph McCarney, *Routledge Philosophy Guidebook to Hegel on History* (London: Routledge, 2000), 173–75.

12. Also see Stephen Houlgate, *An Introduction to Hegel: Freedom, Truth and History* (Malden, MA: Blackwell Publishing, 2005), 4–8; also see Burleigh Taylor Wilkins, *Hegel's Philosophy of History* (Ithaca: Cornell University Press, 1974), 23–28.

13. Hassner, "Hegel," 742.

14. Also see Leo Strauss, "The Three Waves of Modernity," in *An Introduction to Political Philosophy: Ten Essays by Leo Strauss* (Detroit: Wayne State University Press, 1989), 91; McCarney, *Hegel on History*, 158–59; Findlay, *Hegel*, 323; and Marcuse, *Reason and Revolution*, 227, 229.

15. Hassner, "Hegel," 733; also see Findlay, *Hegel*, 322; but see McCarney, *Hegel on History*, 155–56.

16. See McCarney, *Hegel on History*, 46–48.

17. For instance, see Plato, *Apology*, G.M.A. Grube trans. (Indianapolis: Hackett Publishing company, 2002), 28d-29a, 30e-31b, 38a; Plato, *Meno*, G.M.A. Grube trans. (Indianapolis: Hackett Publishing company, 2002), 72b-d; and Plato, *Republic*, Allan Bloom trans. (New York: Basic books, 1969), 517b-c. All subsequent citations of the *Republic* will be taken from this edition.

18. But see Findlay who suggests that World-historical individuals are aware that Spirit is animating their passions and actions, Finlday, *Hegel*, 330. Also see Speight, *Hegel*, 93.

19. Also see Marcuse, *Reason and Revolution*, 233–34.

20. For a similar understanding of how Socrates undermines confidence in the reigning values of society, see Pierre Hadot, *What Is Ancient Philosophy?*, Michael Chase trans. (Cambridge: Harvard University Press, 2002), 28–29, 36–37.

21. See Michael Inwood, *Hegel*, (Abingdon, Oxon: Routledge, 1983), 506.

Chapter Two

Abraham and Socrates

Love and History in Kierkegaard's Fear and Trembling

In the Introduction to the *Philosophy of History,* Hegel argues that Spirit, or the universality of reason, is fully actualized when the modern liberal state emerges, and thus humanity and history reach their end and perfection. Such perfection requires that the individual become subsumed within the state by internalizing the rational laws of the state. Shedding their particularity for unity within the whole, persons attain freedom from the individuating constraints of the body and its passions, transforming themselves into thinking rather than feeling beings. Moreover, such perfection at the end of history means there can be no appeal to something beyond modern law and politics to critique such modern law and politics. Socratic skepticism, therefore, which questions the authoritative opinions of the political community in search of higher truths, as it were, should cease when the modern state comes into being.

In *Fear and Trembling* Søren Kierkegaard, through his pseudonym "Johannes de Silentio" or "John of Silence," argues that if we in liberal modernity have achieved the highest so that humanity has been perfected and history has come to an end, then there is nothing left for us to do (*FT* 119–23).[1] Human greatness, as Hegel suggests, disappears, because all difficult but beautiful tasks to inspire noble youths have ceased. What does Kierkegaard suggest these tasks are? Kierkegaard, in contrast to Hegel's deification of reason, believes "the essentially human is passion" and hence the highest task is to love. The problem in liberal modernity, therefore, is that we moderns have forgotten how to love. Kierkegaard will seek to remind us of what it means to love by providing models of human greatness who pursued this noble task. Since, for Kierkegaard, "the highest passion in a

27

person is faith," the greatest love is the love of God. Abraham, therefore, as the father of faith, is the foremost model of human greatness that Kierkegaard presents in *Fear and Trembling*. However, Kierkegaard maintains that very few individuals in any generation can experience the faith of Abraham. Yet, Kierkegaard also maintains that there are other forms of love which are analogous to but differ from faith. The most important of these is Socratic philosophy. Thus, I argue that as Kierkegaard's work concludes, we realize that *Fear and Trembling*, which began as eulogy to Abraham and the life of faith, is actually a eulogy to Socrates and the philosophic life.

Kierkegaard, therefore, in contradistinction to Hegel who argues for its end, presents Socratic philosophy as crucial for human flourishing in liberal modernity. Moreover, Kierkegaard presents the greatness of Socrates and that of Abraham as attained by transcending and even violating the rational moral order of one's political community. Kierkegaard, therefore, pushes back against Hegel's call for the absorption of the individual into the state at what the latter believes is the end of history. Rather, in presenting Abraham and Socrates as models of human greatness for noble individuals in liberal modernity to emulate, Kierkegaard encourages such individuals to transcend the modern state and the bounds of their time, and possibly even reason itself, thereby ensuring that history and human greatness not disappear.

Merold Westphal argues, in contrast, that Kierkegaard does not understand Abraham or the person of faith as transcending reason and morality as such, or "the historically unmediated ethics of pure reason," but rather as appealing to a higher "Moral Law" above and beyond the particular laws and customs or "prevailing social practices" of one's particular and historically situated nation, state, society, or people.[2] Thus, for Kierkegaard, according to Westphal, there is no real conflict between reason and revelation or morality and faith.[3]

I believe, however, that there are two problems with Westphal's argument that faith, for Kierkegaard, which requires transcending one's society or state, does not also require movement beyond reason. First, although Hegel contends that in all previous epochs Spirit, or what Westphal calls "pure reason" or the "Moral Law," is only partially revealed and thus always historically situated, he also contends that Spirit or universal reason and morality as such, does indeed become fully revealed and actualized at the end of history in the modern liberal state. Thus, there is no appeal beyond this state to a higher "Moral Law," as it were. Yet, it is precisely noble youths in this modern liberal state to whom Kierkegaard appeals with the model of Abraham and his transcendence of his moral and social order. Second, in choosing to discuss Abraham and the story of his intention to kill Isaac in obedience to God's command, it is reasonable to assume that Kierkegaard is looking to an absolute moral standard—the abstention from murder, especially the murder of one's child—that applies to all human communities and which is open to human reason regardless of space and time, to illustrate his understanding of what faith is and what the biblical God sometimes requires. Thus, it is hard to support the argument that Kierkegaard understands Abraham's intentions, or faith as such, as simply an adherence to a higher, more rational moral standard external to one's own social and historical situation.[4]

ABRAHAM AND THE IMPLICIT CHALLENGE TO HEGEL

Kierkegaard challenges Hegel's understanding of the unfolding of history and human perfection in reason at the end of history in the modern liberal state, initially by presenting Abraham, the father of faith, as an alternative model of human greatness. Kierkegaard, in his "Eulogy on Abraham," praises "Venerable Father Abraham! Second Father of the race!" as being the greatest of human beings (*FT* 23, 16). Thus, Kierkegaard's mere choice of subject matter in Abraham itself stands as a broad critique of Hegel's understanding of history and human perfection. Abraham, the model of human perfection, is presented by Kierkegaard as the second Adam and thus near the beginning of time, rather than at its end. Kierkegaard therefore calls into question Hegel's claim that human perfection comes at the end of history, and thus he also calls into question Hegel's thesis that history is a rational and divine process in which Spirit gradually unfolds itself until it becomes fully disclosed in concrete form in the modern liberal state.

Abraham's perfection, moreover, is grounded in his love, not his reason. Human greatness, according to Kierkegaard, is measured in proportion to the greatness of that which we love, but Abraham "loved God and became the greatest of all" (*FT* 16). Kierkegaard thus immediately raises the question of the nature of God. For Abraham, in contrast to Hegel, "God is love," not thought. Thus, whereas Hegel's God is concerned with "Peoples" or "Totalities that are states," Abraham's God is radically concerned with the particular or with individual human beings. God's providence is particular, not just general. Abraham, therefore, perfects himself not because he, in the Hegelian sense, thinks about thought itself, or the universal, but because he, in loving God, loves love itself, or the ultimate particular (*FT* 34). Thus, whereas Hegel's perfect human being at the end of history thinks or grasps the universal, Abraham loves or grasps the particular.

In grasping at the particular, Kierkegaard suggests that Abraham imitates his God, who, as love, "is concerned about the smallest things" (*FT* 34). Abraham's love for or faith in such a God, allows him to expect the impossible or the unreasonable, which, according to Kierkegaard, sets off a sequence of events in Abraham's life which makes him "the greatest of all" (*FT* 16). Kierkegaard claims that Abraham's love for God, or his faith, allowed him to receive God's promise that he and Sarah would have a son in their old age, and that through this son all the generations of the earth would be blessed (*FT* 18; see also *Genesis* 18, 22). Abraham's faith, however, not only allowed him to receive God's promise, but it also allowed him to receive and resist God's temptation. After Isaac, the promised son, was born, God called to Abraham, and said "Abraham, Abraham, where are you?" And Abraham answered, "Here am I" (*FT* 21). Then, according to Kierkegaard, "God tempted Abraham and said to him, take Isaac, your only son, whom you love, and go to the land of Moriah and offer him as a burnt offering on a mountain that I shall show you" (*FT* 19; see also *Genesis* 22).

The nature of the temptation which God places before Abraham is not the temptation to be lax in performing one's moral duty toward others in the pursuit of one's own selfish desires. Rather, the temptation is precisely to do one's moral duty toward others, in this case the father's duty towards the son. According to Kierkegaard, "There is no higher expression for the ethical in Abraham's life than that the father shall love the son" (*FT* 59). Abraham is tempted by God to act ethically; not to kill or sacrifice his son—rather than to obey God's unethical command. Thus, Kierkegaard says that, "As a rule, what tempts a person is something that will hold him back from doing his duty, but here the temptation is the ethical itself; which would hold him back from doing God's will" (*FT* 60). Hence, will Abraham hold the ethical to be God, as Hegel does? Or, in other words, will Abraham hold that God is bound or constrained by the moral rules that inhere between human beings and thereby deify the ethical or moral order?

Abraham, Kierkegaard suggests, resists the temptation to deify the ethical or moral order. Responding promptly and without doubt to God's command, Abraham set off for Mount Moriah, traveled in silence for three days, and then on the fourth day he ascended the mountain, arranged the firewood, bound Isaac, and lifted the knife with full intent to sacrifice him (*FT* 12, 21). By his intent to sacrifice Isaac, Abraham shows that he loves a God who, as love, is beyond the moral order, and who can thereby command its violation; that the father shall kill the son. However, this command produces the passion of dread and anxiety in Abraham, as it places him at odds with his ethical obligations and condemns him to silence (*FT* 21, 28). Abraham cannot communicate God's command and his intent to sacrifice Isaac to anyone. Even if he did speak to Sarah, his servant Eliezer, or even to Isaac himself, he would not be able to make himself understood and thus remains totally isolated (*FT* 10, 21). Moreover, in intending to sacrifice Isaac, Abraham makes what Kierkegaard calls the "movement of infinity" or "infinite resignation," by which one gives up the particular object of one's love for the sake of God, or negates the finite for the infinite (*FT* 35–38). Abraham, however, in making this movement, not only gives up his son, but the nation or future generations within his son as well.

Abraham, although he makes this movement of infinite resignation whereby he intends to sacrifice Isaac and the nation within Isaac, also believes he will not have to. According to Kierkegaard, Abraham believed that at the same time God demanded the sacrifice of Isaac, God would also keep his promise to him and not require the sacrifice of Isaac. According to Kierkegaard, Abraham believed "God could give him a new Isaac, could restore to life the one sacrificed" (*FT* 36). Abraham's faith is for this life and not for a reward in the next. Thus, Abraham has faith not only in a God who transcends the moral order, but in a God who transcends the natural and hence temporal order as well. Abraham believes that God can intervene in the universal laws which govern nature and time, and allow Isaac to live and die, to be and not be, at the same time. Abraham, in believing in such a God, makes a second movement, the "movement of finitude," whereby one believes that one will get the sacrificed particularity back again; "one does not lose the finite but gains it whole and intact" (*FT* 37). This movement, which Kierkegaard says is the movement of faith, is made "by virtue of the absurd," and thus is completely beyond the power of human reason to comprehend. In moving back to the finite after having sacrificed it, Abraham moves beyond the rational and must rely on the power of God. Yet, Abraham's powerlessness is his strength. According to Kierkegaard, by acknowledging his limits as a rational human being in the face of a limitless and loving divine being, Abraham actually conquers God and becomes the greatest of all human beings (*FT* 16). In the very last moment, God repents of his demand for Isaac and makes a ram appear for Abraham to sacrifice instead (*FT* 12, 22).

As the father of faith, Kierkegaard eulogizes Abraham as the first to "feel and bear witness to that prodigious passion that disdains the terrifying battle with the elements and the forces of creation in order to contend with God" (*FT* 23). Kierkegaard indicates that faith induces the greatest of passions. This passion occurs when one is placed outside both the moral and natural orders by a God who, as love, is also beyond both the moral and natural orders. As a passion, this experience of being placed outside both the ethical and natural orders and thereby coming closer to God Himself, can only be felt, not known. Thus, Kierkegaard declares, "I cannot think myself into Abraham" (*FT* 33). Faith is fundamentally irrational.

In the "Preliminary Expectoration," Kierkegaard gives what he believes is a more readily accessible illustration of the two movements of Abraham by presenting what he calls a "love affair" between a young lad and a princess. However, not only does this "love affair" make Abraham's two movements more accessible to the reader in an intellectual sense, but it also presents them in a very apolitical light. Kierkegaard suggests how one can become a "knight of faith" or emulate the greatness of Abraham in modernity, even if one remains solely within the private sphere.

The love affair begins when the young lad falls in love with the princess, and, putting "the entire substance of his life" into his love for the beloved, "feels a blissful delight in letting love palpitate in every nerve" (*FT* 41–42). Thus, Kierkegaard indicates that romantic love at first excites and delights the senses, and thus allows the lover to take pleasure in feeling his own body or individual existence as a material, finite being. However, the next stage in the affair occurs when the young lad learns that his love for the princess is an "impossibility"; perhaps she is too high-born for him and thus that he will never marry the princess or consummate his love for her (*FT* 42). The young lad, Kierkegaard indicates, then makes the movement of infinite resignation (*FT* 42). In making this movement, the young lad, just as Abraham gives up Isaac, gives up his love for the particular or finite princess. Yet, in giving up his love for the finite princess, he does not therefore abandon his love, but transforms or sublimates it into love for the "eternal being" or idea of the princess. According to Kierkegaard, "His love for that princess would become for him the expression of an eternal love . . . would be transfigured into a love of the eternal being, which true enough denied the fulfillment but nevertheless did reconcile him once more in the eternal consciousness of its validity in an eternal form that no actuality can take away from him" (*FT* 43).

From the moment the young lad makes this movement of infinite resignation and exchanges his love for the finite for a love for the infinite, Kierkegaard claims that "the princess is lost" (*FT* 44). The idea of the beloved, Kierkegaard suggests, will always be superior to the particular or finite beloved. Moreover, because this idea is internal to the lover, once gained the presence of the finite beloved which spawned it is no longer needed to sustain it. The young lad "does not need the erotic titillation of seeing his beloved etc.," and in fact, the young lad "has grasped the deep secret that even in loving another person one ought to be sufficient onto oneself. He is no longer concerned about what the finite princess does, and precisely this proves that has made the movement infinitely" (*FT* 44). Kierkegaard indicates that the lack of consummation of love for the finite tends to intensify love, whereas consummation causes love to dissipate. Ironically, therefore, romantic love, if it is to be sustained, cannot bring two finite beings together, but requires that they remain apart. They cannot love each other as particular beings, but only as eternal or "ideal" beings.

Kierkegaard indicates that the young lad, in making the movement of infinite resignation, discovers his own "eternal consciousness" (*FT* 48). What Kierkegaard means here is that he becomes conscious of the fact that as a human being, he is conscious of possessing not just a body, which is finite and particular to the self, but also a soul, which is infinite or one with the universal.[5] The soul is understood as one with the universal, because it can grasp or tend toward universal principles or ideas which transcend finite particulars, such as the idea of the princess rather than the princess herself.

Thus, in discovering his "eternal consciousness" in infinite resignation, the young lad, like Hegel and those human beings he says perfect themselves in the modern state, becomes conscious of his soul as mind or reason, which always tends toward universality rather than particularity or individuation. Kierkegaard suggests that in transforming his love for the princess into a love for the idea or "eternal being" of the princess, the young lad actually transforms his love, originally grounded in the body and its passions, into thought, which is located in the soul. When one grasps at the universal, one thinks; only when one grasps at the particular does one love. Thus, for Kierkegaard, the young lad's act of resignation does not require faith, because it is "a merely philosophical movement" (*FT* 48).

The young lad only becomes a proper analogy to Abraham and therefore a knight of faith, by making one more movement, absent in Hegel's scheme, after the movement of infinite resignation, the movement of finitude. The young lad becomes a knight of faith when, according to Kierkegaard:

> He does exactly the same as the other knight did: he infinitely renounces the love that is the substance of his life, he is reconciled in pain. But then the marvel happens; he makes one more movement even more wonderful than all the others, for he says: Nevertheless I have faith that I will get her—that is, by virtue of the absurd, by virtue of the fact that for God all things are possible (*FT* 46).

Thus, like Abraham, who believes that God will restore Isaac to him at the same time that he sacrifices him, the young lad moves back to the finite princess after having sacrificed her, because he believes that for God (the absurd or that which is beyond reason) all things are possible. Yet, as Kierkegaard argues, God is love, and thus, in believing that for God all things are possible, the young lad believes that for love (the absurd or that which is beyond reason) all things are possible. [6] By becoming a lover of God, he will once more become a lover of the finite princess and get her back again.

In making the movement of finitude after the movement of infinite resignation, Kierkegaard indicates that the young lad becomes conscious of the fact that although he is a soul which is rational, this soul can embrace the finite as well as the infinite, the particular as well as the universal; he can love the finite princess as well as the idea he has of her at the same time. Why? Because the soul is not just reason but also love, it can feel as well as think. The soul does not just have thoughts but also passions; there are passions of the soul which are not simply passions of the body. Thus, the young lad can derive his individual identity or separateness from the universal, not just from his material existence and all things connected with it, but from his soul or his immaterial existence as well. He gains a higher individuality based in the passions of the soul in contradistinction to a lower individuality based in the passions of the body. [7] Kierkegaard suggests that both the young lad in love with the princess and Abraham, in making the movement of faith, unite what he regards as the two parts of the soul, reason and passion or thought and love, with passion and love understood as higher than reason and thought. In doing so, the knight of faith, the greatest of human beings, transcends the human perfection that Hegel regards as becoming completely actualized at the end of history.

By referencing the passions of the soul by which the knight of faith grounds a higher individuality, I am introducing a Platonic conception of the soul into the analysis. For instance, in book 4 of Plato's *Republic*, Socrates considers the structure of the human soul, specifically whether or not it has three distinct parts. According to Socrates, to discover if this is true is, "hard to determine in a way worthy of the argument" (*Rep* 436b). Socrates asks:

> Do we act in each of these ways as a result of the same part of ourselves, or are there three parts and with a different one we act in each of the different ways? Do we learn with one, become spirited with another of the parts within us, and desire the pleasures of nourishment and generation and all their kin with a third; or do we act with the soul as a whole in each of them once we are started? (*Rep* 436a–b)

In the above passage Socrates asks his interlocutors to consider two alternatives with regard to the structure of the soul. First, it is possible that the soul is without parts. In this case, the whole soul would desire at one time, and then it would turn and the whole soul would be spirited at one time, and turning again the whole soul would learn or think at one time. In other words, a soul without parts means we would "put our all into everything we do," as it were, at any one time. Second, it is possible that the soul possesses distinct parts. In this case, we would desire with one part of the soul, with another we would be spirited, and with another part we would learn or think. Such a divided soul would allow us to be pulled in opposite directions at once, as it were, desiring one thing but being spirited for or thinking another.

Socrates begins his consideration on the second alternative, that the soul possesses distinct parts, by reflecting on whether, "sometimes there are some men who are thirsty but not willing to drink" (*Rep* 439c). Of such persons Socrates suggests:

> Isn't there something in their soul bidding them to drink and something forbidding them to do so, some-thing different that masters that which bids? [. . .] Doesn't that which forbids such things come into being [. . .] from calculation, while what leads and draws is present due to affection and diseases? (*Rep* 439c–d)

With the example of persons both thirsty and unwilling to drink at the same time, Socrates attempts to show that the soul has a distinct rational part—that which forbids the thirsty person from drinking, and a distinct non-rational or desiring part—that which draws the thirsty person to drink (*Rep* 439d–e). Moreover, not only does Socrates bring to light two distinct parts of the soul, but he indicates a hierarchy as well. Socrates suggests that it is the job or function of the rational part of the soul to master or pull back, as it were, the desiring part of the soul. The desires in this discussion have been subordinated to the rule of reason. In my analysis of Kierkegaard's implications with regard to the human soul, Socrates' articulation of the desiring part of the soul in the *Republic* is the framework I use to understand the passions in the soul of knights of faith who believe they will get the finite object of their love back again after having sacrificed it. Socrates' and Kierkegaard's conceptions of the soul differ at this point, however, as Socrates subordinates the desires to reason in contrast to Kierkegaard who elevates them.

Returning to the *Republic*, Socrates argues that reason in the soul will be aided in its rule of desire by spiritedness. Reflecting on whether spiritedness is a distinct part of the soul, Socrates tells the story of Leontius. According to Socrates:

> Leontius [. . .] was going up from the Piraeus under the outside of the North Wall when he noticed corpses lying by the public executioner. He desired to look, but at the same time he was disgusted and made himself turn away: and for a while he struggled and covered his face. But finally, overpowered by the desire, he opened his eyes wide, ran toward the corpses and said: 'Look, you damned wretches, take your fill of the fair sight.' (*Rep* 439e–440a)

The struggle Leontius endures with himself indicates that spiritedness is the source of our sense of shame, or that which causes us to resist that part of ourselves we regard as low and to get angry at ourselves when the lower part gets the upper hand, as it were. The inverse of shame is pride which attempts to hide what is low so that we can appear higher or better than we think we are. Leontius' story points to a number of phenomena that spiritedness regards as low, or that it is ashamed of. One of the most important is human mortality or death. Spiritedness appears disgusted at bodily death, regarding our bodily nature as low or shameful. Spirited disgust at the mortality of the body also sheds light on the nature of the desires that it resists. The desires in this story want to view human mortality or the limits of our bodily nature, perhaps revealing that the desires are aware of and reveal our fundamental incompleteness or lack, pointing to our need of another or something outside of ourselves. Spiritedness, it would seem, hates this incompleteness or deficiency. Despite its proneness to anger and violence, and despite the apparent conclusion to the Leontius story, Socrates says that the ability of spiritedness to resist the desiring part of the soul makes it amenable to reason. Spiritedness, therefore, is the natural "ally" of, though distinct from, the rational part of the soul (*Rep* 440b, 440c–e).

An area of potential concern with the structure of the soul articulated by Socrates is brought to light if we reflect more on the awareness of lack associated with the desires. According to Socrates:

> Being thirsty and hungry and generally the desires [. . .] willing and wanting [. . .] Won't you say that the soul of a man who desires either longs for what it desires or embraces that which it wants to become its own; or again [. . .] insofar as the soul wills that something be supplied to it, it nods assent to itself as though someone had posed a question and reaches out toward fulfillment of what it wills? (*Rep* 437b–c)

As this passage suggests, the desires contain within themselves and bring to us an awareness of our need for something other—either inanimate or animate—outside of the self, together with the longing to embrace this other to make it one's own or part of the self, thus becoming different or other than what we were. Socrates, therefore, suggesting that in the properly structured soul reason with the help of spiritedness resists or suppresses desire, suggests that the just soul, the soul of the guardian and philosopher, is a "closed" or self-contained soul, as it were, unchanging as it sealed off from the world outside of itself. This problematic character of the just soul as it appears in book 4 also comes to light, as we shall see below, in the discussion in book 5 of the third "wave."

At the beginning of book 5 of the *Republic*, Socrates' interlocutors want him to clarify an assertion he made in passing that as for women and children in the just city, "the things of friends will be in common" (*Rep* 449c, 424a). Socrates, responding that, "it would be right [. . .] after having completely finished the male drama to complete the female," indicates what was not clear prior to this interruption in book 5, namely that women must now enter the city in speech, having been absent before (*Rep* 451c). Women enter the city in what Socrates characterizes as "waves": the first is the equality of the sexes in which women are given the same education in preparation for doing the same jobs as men, and the second, the abolition of the private family in favor of common wives and the communal possession and rearing of children (*Rep* 457b).

The third wave, "the biggest and most difficult," according to Socrates, enters the city in response to Glaucon's question of what will make it possible for their just city, including the equality of the sexes and the communism of women and children, to come into being. According to Socrates, the just city, or the closest approximation to it that would be practically possible, would only come into being if, "the philosophers ruled as kings or those now called kings and chiefs genuinely and adequately philosophize, and political power and philosophy coincide in the same place" (*Rep* 473d). It seems that only with the female drama, or with the entry of women into the city, do we get the philosophic drama, or the entry of philosophers into the city.

Glaucon indicates how difficult it would be for philosophy to come to power when he says that most people hate philosophers and would rather kill them than see them rule (*Rep* 474a). Socrates, however, proceeds to clarify for Glaucon who the philosophers actually are, claiming that this hostility to philosophy is due to the common inability to distinguish the "true lover of learning" from the many non-philosophers who call themselves such (*Rep* 474b–c, 475c). Socrates begins his clarification by arguing that, since the philosopher is a "lover of learning," to know who the philosopher is we must first know what it means, in the precise sense, for an erotic person to love (*Rep* 474c–d). If the philosopher is fundamentally the most erotic of persons, as Socrates now suggests, the philosopher's soul now seems unlike the soul of book 4. The soul in book 4 is a "closed" soul, with reason ruling spiritedness and with the help of spiritedness pulling the desires back or holding them in check against things outside of itself. In book 5, however, the philosopher is a "lover of learning" and thus the most erotic of persons.[8] It would seem, therefore, that within the philosophic soul reason and desire (and spiritedness) are mixed or operating in tandem, moving as one, like the soul without parts, toward an object of love. In this sense the philosopher has an "open" soul, being drawn to objects of longing thought outside of the self.

The open and longing soul of the philosopher articulated by Socrates in book 5 of the *Republic*, more closely resembles the soul of the knight of faith in Kierkegaard's *Fear and Trembling*. They differ, however, in that Socrates' philosopher will long for universal ideas culminating in the most universal idea of the good, whereas Abraham will have a passion in his soul for the ultimate particular beyond the universal. As a result, it seems, Kierkegaard's implications with regard to the soul still imply a soul with parts with desires (or passions) as the highest part.

ABRAHAM AND THE TRAGIC HERO: THE EXPLICIT CHALLENGE TO HEGEL

Kierkegaard proceeds to make his challenge to Hegel explicit by asking three questions about the story of Abraham, each of which form the title of three different "Problemata." Moreover, at the beginning of each "Problemata," Kierkegaard gives what he regards is a Hegelian account of the ethical which fails to comprehend faith, and thus fundamentally misunderstands the highest in human life. Here we shall focus on the first two "Problemata," in which Kierkegaard illustrates Hegel's failure to grasp the highest, by contrasting Abraham with the "tragic hero." This is a much more political presentation of Abraham, and thus in his explicit challenge to Hegel, Kierkegaard makes much more apparent the political significance of what it means to emulate the greatness of Abraham or to become a knight of faith.

In "Problema I," Kierkegaard asks with respect to Abraham, "Is there a Teleological Suspension of the Ethical?" Before answering this question, Kierkegaard proceeds to give an account of what he means by the ethical. First, the ethical is the universal and thus, in the Hegelian context, it is the rational. As the universal and rational, Kierkegaard maintains that the ethical applies to everyone at all times (*FT* 54).[9] Kierkegaard, therefore, unlike Hegel, suggests that there are absolute moral standards of rational behavior, the full manifestation of which transcend time and space. The second characteristic with which Kierkegaard endows the ethical is its comprehensiveness or perfection. The ethical, according to Kierkegaard, "has nothing outside itself that is its 'telos' [end, purpose] but is itself the 'telos' for everything outside itself, and when the ethical has absorbed this into itself, it goes no further" (*FT* 54). Thus, the single individual, "sensately and physically qualified in immediacy," has his end in the universal, and his "ethical task" is to "annul his singularity in order to become the universal" (*FT* 54). For Kierkegaard, the single individual, "sensately and physically qualified in immediacy," is the "esthetic" individual, or an individual who derives his particularity or individual identity from the body and the selfish passions to which it gives rise (*FT* 82). The esthetic individual in Hegel's terms is "Matter." When the esthetic individual completes his ethical task and becomes one with the universal, he sheds his individual identity based in the passions of the body, for a common or universal identity based in the soul understood as mind. In Hegel's terms, he becomes "Spirit."

Kierkegaard, moreover, calls the ethical "social morality" (*FT* 55). By doing so, he identifies the ethical, as Westphal notes, with the rational moral and social order embodied by the nation, state, society, or people.[10] In this case, when the esthetic individual completes his ethical task, he exchanges his private passionate will for the universal and hence rational will of the political community; he wills the universal. He thereby negates his particularity for universality or transforms himself from a feeling being governed by the body and its passions, into a thinking being governed by the rational part of the soul. From an isolated and selfish individual he becomes a completely socialized member of his community.

Kierkegaard indicates that he has given an account of the ethical which he believes is consistent with Hegelian philosophy. He thus generally concedes the accuracy of Hegel's understanding of this phenomenon, with the qualification that for Kierkegaard, there are rational and hence ethical moral standards that transcend time or historical context. Yet, Kierkegaard indicates that if the ethical is for Hegel the highest form of existence, then there can be no teleological suspension of the ethical, or nothing higher than the ethical that would justify its violation. If Hegel is right, then Abraham must be condemned as a murderer rather than praised as the father of faith (*FT* 55). Why? Because, according to Kierkegaard:

> Faith is namely this paradox that the single individual is higher than the universal—yet, please note, in such a way that the movement repeats itself, so that after having been in the universal he as the single individual isolates himself as higher than the universal. If this is not faith then Abraham is lost. (*FT* 55)

Abraham, therefore, sheds his esthetic individuality to move through the universal, but then goes beyond it to regain a higher individuality that transcends both reason and morality. Yet, Kierkegaard maintains that for Hegel and most other ethical persons, "As soon as the individual asserts himself in his singularity before the universal, he sins," or falls below the ethical into the esthetic rather than rising above the ethical and entering the paradox of faith (*FT* 54). Why? Because Hegel, unlike Abraham, deifies the ethical, and thus must answer Kierkegaard's second question about the Abraham story in the negative.

In "Problema II," Kierkegaard asks, "Is there an Absolute Duty to God?" Again, before answering this question, Kierkegaard gives what he believes is an Hegelian account of the ethical in which "The ethical is the universal, and as such it is divine" (*FT* 68). The consequence of such an understanding of the ethical is to deny any direct or absolute duties to God beyond those contained in the rational moral law upheld by one's society or political community (*FT* 68).[11] Hegel absolutizes the ethical or collapse the distinction between God and the rational moral and social order embodied by the community, and faith simply becomes proper socialization within that order.[12] Thus, one can never enter into a personal or private relationship with God that transcends one's society, because, as Kierkegaard maintains, in doing one's social duty, for example "to love one's neighbor," one enters into a relation with one's neighbor, not with God (*FT* 68).

Kierkegaard, however, claims that if Hegel was right in deifying the ethical, "he was not right in speaking about faith or in permitting Abraham to be regarded as its father" (*FT* 68). Again, Hegel cannot comprehend faith, because, according to Kierkegaard:

> The paradox of faith, then, is this: that the single individual [. . .] determines his relation to the universal by his relation to the absolute (God), not his relation to the absolute by his relation to the universal. The paradox may also be expressed in this way: that there is an absolute duty to God, for in this relationship of duty the individual relates himself as the single individual absolutely to the absolute. (*FT* 70)

Thus, whereas Hegel absolutizes or deifies the ethical, Abraham relativizes the ethical by placing the absolute, or God, above it. Because Abraham believes that God, as love, transcends the ethical, he can show an absolute or direct duty to God unmediated by the universal or his rational duties toward other human beings. In other words, Abraham can enter into a personal or private relationship with God by violating his relationships with or duties toward other people. By doing so, Abraham enters the paradox of faith whereby "the single individual as the single individual is higher than the universal" (*FT* 55).

Moreover, at the beginning of "Problema II," Kierkegaard argues that Hegel associates the esthetic with the "inner" or "interiority," by which he means something similar to privacy and individuation, and the ethical with the "external" or "exteriority," by which he means something similar to a publicity and socialization (*FT* 69). For Hegel, exteriority is higher than interiority, and thus the ethical task of the esthetic individual is to rise above his essentially private individual life and enter into a proper public or social life. Yet again, Kierkegaard indicates that Hegel has misunderstood faith because, "The paradox of faith is that there is an interiority that is incommensurable with exteriority, an interiority that is not identical, please note, with the first but is a new interiority" (*FT* 69).

Kierkegaard illustrates how Hegel's understanding of the ethical cannot comprehend faith, and therefore the highest in human life, by contrasting Abraham with those whom he identifies as "tragic heroes."[13] The archetypal tragic hero for Kierkegaard is Agamemnon, who, to appease the angry gods and obtain a favorable wind for his fleet to sail to Troy, must sacrifice his daughter Iphigenia and thereby save "an enterprise of concern to the whole nation" (*FT* 57–58). In doing so he suffers great agony, but touches the souls and inspires admiration and compassion in his people and all others who remember him. According to Kierkegaard, "there will never be a noble soul in the world without tears of compassion for (his) agony, of admiration for (his) deed" (*FT* 58).

The tragic hero, therefore, must sacrifice his child to save the nation. In doing so, he makes the movement of infinite resignation whereby he sacrifices the particular, in the form of his child, for the universal, in the form of the nation, or the rational moral and social order embodied by the nation. However, in sacrificing his child, the tragic hero in a way sacrifices himself or his own esthetic individuality—his child is flesh from his flesh, flesh and the selfish passions to which it gives rise being particular to the individual. Thus, in making the movement of infinite resignation, the tragic hero "relinquishes himself to express the universal" (*FT* 75). By doing so, Kierkegaard argues that "every individual who understands him in turn understands the universal in him, and both rejoice in the security of the universal" (*FT* 75). Thus, the tragic hero not only expresses or grasps the universality of his own particular nation, but of the nation or country as such. One can only be a rational and hence moral being within a community, or by allowing the universal will to take precedence over one's merely esthetic or selfish individual will, shedding one's individual identity for a common or universal identity. The tragic hero therefore, completes his ethical task, and although he suspends the ethical obligation to his child, he does so "without moving beyond the teleology of the ethical" (*FT* 57)[14] In the case of the tragic hero, according to Kierkegaard, there is no teleological suspension of the ethical.

The tragic hero, because he remains within the ethical, does not enter into a personal or private relationship to the divine unmediated by the universal or his ethical duties toward other human beings. Why? Because the ethical, according to Kierkegaard, which applies to all men at all times, "is the divine" for the tragic hero (*FT* 60). The tragic hero, in sacrificing his child to save the nation, only enters into a direct relation with other men, not the divine. He does not show an absolute duty to God which transcends his allegiance to the nation, but rather shows an absolute duty to the nation which he believes comprehends the divine. The tragic hero is therefore, for Kierkegaard, a very Hegelian hero.

Kierkegaard's presentation of the tragic hero is similar to what he believes is the Hegelian presentation of human perfection at the end of history. Like the human beings who perfect themselves in Hegel's modern state at the end of history, the tragic hero completes his ethical task of annulling his esthetic singularity to become one with the universal.[15] Thus, in sacrificing his child to save the nation, the tragic hero negates esthetic individuality to enter the ethical or universal, and thereby replaces his private passionate will with the universal and hence rational will of the community. He thereby transforms himself from a feeling being guided by the passions of the body, into a thinking being guided by reason or the soul understood as mind. In doing so, he sheds his individual identity for a common identity, and exchanges his private interior life for a fully socialized exterior or public life. The tragic hero, therefore, becomes fully transparent or known by others.

Abraham differs from the tragic hero in significant ways. The tragic hero sacrifices his child to save the nation, and thus makes the movement of infinite resignation whereby he completes his ethical task of negating his esthetic particularity, in the form of his child, for the sake of the universal, in the form of the nation. Abraham, on the other hand, also makes the movement of infinite resignation, but with the qualification that Abraham, unlike the tragic hero, in sacrificing or intending to sacrifice Isaac, also sacrifices the nation or the universal that is within Isaac. Thus, whereas the tragic hero sacrifices the particular for the universal, Abraham sacrifices both the particular and the universal. According to Kierkegaard:

> There is no higher expression for the ethical in Abraham's life than that the father shall love the son. The ethical in the sense of the moral is entirely beside the point. Insofar as the universal was present, it was cryptically in Isaac, hidden so to speak in Isaac's loins, and must cry out with Isaac's mouth: Do not do this, you are destroying everything. (*FT* 59)

Thus, unlike the tragic hero who remains within the ethical, Abraham moves completely beyond it and acts as an isolated individual outside of and higher than the universal. In the case of Abraham, there is indeed a teleological suspension of the ethical (*FT* 59, 61). Thus, whereas the tragic hero "relinquishes himself to express the universal," Abraham "gives up the universal to grasp something higher that is not universal" (*FT* 60, 75). This higher particularity that Abraham attempts to grasp is his God, who, as love, according to Kierkegaard, "is the one who demands absolute love" (*FT* 73). Real love, Kierkegaard suggests, is always exclusive or tends radically toward the particular. Thus, if Abraham is to show that he is truly a lover of God, he cannot share his love between his family, his nation, and his God, but Abraham must show an allegiance or duty to God that is beyond his family and nation by sacrificing Isaac and the nation that is within Isaac.[16] Unlike the tragic hero, for whom the ethical or the universal is divine, for Abraham, God, as love, is beyond the ethical or the universal, and thus can demand its violation.

The God of Abraham, however, as love, does not just transcend the moral order or the universal ethical laws that adhere between human beings, but He also transcends the natural and temporal order, or the universal laws which govern nature and time. God can make Isaac be and not be at the same time, or can raise Isaac from the dead. Thus, at the same time that Abraham makes the movement of infinite resignation, he makes one movement more which the tragic hero does not make, the movement of finitude, whereby he believes he will receive Isaac back again after having sacrificed him.[17] According to Kierkegaard, Abraham had faith that "God could give him a new Isaac, could restore to life the one sacrificed." The particular, therefore, which Abraham attempts to grasp, thereby proving himself to be a lover, is not just his God, who is higher than the universal, but also his son, in whom the universal was only cryptically present.

In making these two movements, Abraham moves completely beyond the ethical or universal, and therefore, unlike the tragic hero, beyond the bounds of what human reason can comprehend. He is thus condemned to silence. Kierkegaard claims that Abraham cannot speak because, as speech expresses the universal but Abraham "has no higher expression of the universal that ranks above the universal that he violates," even if he did try to speak, or express his God and his love for this God, he could not make himself understood.[18] Moreover, Kierkegaard indicates that his utter isolation, which accompanies the inability to communicate the highest with other human beings, induces Abraham to experience painful feelings of anxiety and dread. However, if Abraham experiences the anxiety and dread of being completely isolated from other human beings, he also experiences, according to Kierkegaard, "the wondrous glory the knight attains in becoming God's confidant, the Lord's friend . . . in saying 'You' to God in heaven, whereas even the tragic hero addresses him only in the third person."[19]

Abraham, therefore, by sacrificing both Isaac and the nation within Isaac, isolates himself as a single individual above the universal, and, unlike the tragic hero, he enters into a personal or private relationship with God. By grasping at the particular which is beyond the universal, Kierkegaard indicates that Abraham himself regains a higher particularity or individuality above the universal, or feels a higher passion of the soul in contradistinction to a lower passion of the body. By acquiring this higher individual identity based in the passions of the soul rather than the lower passions of the body, Abraham, transcending the ethical, regains a higher individual and passionate will which he asserts against the universal and hence rational will of the community (in Abraham's case his family and the nation which will proceed from his family). He thereby acquires a new interiority or a higher privacy and individuation above the rational and moral order embodied by his community. Abraham, therefore, unlike the tragic hero, learns that the soul can feel as well as think, or is heart as well as mind. Abraham unites what Kierkegaard implies are the two parts of the soul, passion and reason or love and thought, with passion and love understood as the highest part of the soul. Abraham, however, in becoming a lover and leaving thought, and thus his family and nation, behind, becomes opaque to others rather than transparent. Reason cannot grasp passion, or speech cannot communicate love.

BRINGING THE FEMININE BACK IN

Kierkegaard, by presenting Abraham as elevating the passions of the soul above the mind or reason of the soul, articulates a notion of heroism that brings the claims of the feminine back in at a higher level, claims that were denied by the tragic hero. Kierkegaard points to this problem with the type of heroism embodied by the tragic hero, and thus with Hegel's notion of human perfection at the end of history or in the modern state as well, when he claims, especially in the case of Agamemnon, that there will never be a "noble soul" who does not admire and sanction his deed. Clytemnestra is clearly not within this category of people. Agamemnon is certainly no hero to her. Rather than rejoicing in his deed, Clytemnestra, on his return from Troy, kills her husband in revenge for his sacrifice of their daughter.[20] Thus, Clytemnestra denies the claim which the nation or community makes to be higher than the family or the individual, and thus denies the claim of the ethical that the esthetic individual has his or her end in the universal. Kierkegaard indicates that the tears which both Clytemnestra and Iphigenia shed upon learning of Agamemnon's intentions, show their attachment to esthetic or private existence in contradistinction to Agamemnon's attachment to a political or ethical existence (*FT* 87). Kierkegaard suggests that both Hegel and the tragic hero, by deifying the ethical or the nation, and thereby elevating reason over passion or the universal over the particular, deny the claims of mothers and daughters or of women in general. Thus, by providing Abraham as a model of human greatness which transcends that of the tragic hero, Kierkegaard articulates a notion of heroism that makes room for both men and women, or brings the feminine back in at a higher level. Women as well as men can experience the faith of Abraham and thereby attain human greatness. Kierkegaard illustrates this by describing many feminine models of faith which rival that of Abraham.[21] One of the most prominent of these women is the Virgin Mary, discussed near the end of "Problema I."

Kierkegaard asks with respect to the Virgin Mary, "Who was as great in the world as that favored woman, the mother of God, the Virgin Mary?" (*FT* 65). Mary, Kierkegaard suggests, is a fitting analogy for Abraham who, as the father of faith, was the greatest of all. Kierkegaard indicates that Mary is similar to Abraham, because she believes in a God who wishes her to violate the ethical or to give birth to a child which is not her husband's (*FT* 65). Like Abraham her God is beyond the ethical and moral order and thus can intervene in it and will its violation. Moreover, Mary loves a God who can violate the natural order, or cause her to give birth to a child without ever having been with a man (*FT* 65). Like Abraham, her God is beyond the universal laws that govern nature, and thus can intervene in it and overturn them. Thus, in obeying God's will and becoming "the handmaid of the lord," Mary, like Abraham, stands as a single individual higher than the universal, and enters into a personal or private relationship with God (*FT* 65). In doing so, she, like Abraham, feels the "anxiety and distress" of not being able to make herself understood by anyone: "the angel went only to Mary, and no one could understand her" (*FT* 65). She cannot speak, and if she does, she is unintelligible. Furthermore, Kierkegaard says that although Mary "bore the child miraculously [. . .] she nevertheless did it 'after the manner of women,' and such a time is one of anxiety, distress, and paradox" (*FT* 65).

Kierkegaard, in referring to Mary's having bore her child "after the manner of women," means that she bore her child in pain and suffering. This is a time of anxiety and distress which accompanies entering the paradox of faith, or entering into a personal or private relationship with God, because such painful childbirth, as Kierkegaard alludes to, is due to God's punishment of Eve, and thus to divine intervention in the moral and natural order.[22] Yet, this punishment which God lays on Eve applies to all women, not just Mary. Thus, Kierkegaard indicates that all mothers, when giving birth to their children in pain and suffering enter into a personal or private relationship with God. All mothers, and not just Mary, are examples of faith and human greatness.

In his first two "Problemata," Kierkegaard presents two models of heroism for noble youths in liberal modernity to emulate, the tragic hero and the father of faith. If they choose to emulate the tragic hero, they need look no higher than the ethical or the rational moral and social order embodied by their state as Hegel understands it to have come to be at the end of history. Taking their political community and its laws as their end, these noble youths must complete their ethical task of negating their esthetic particularity to enter the universal, and thereby replace their private passionate will with the universal and hence rational will of the community. In thus becoming model citizens, they will no longer be feeling beings guided by the passions derived from the body, but thinking beings guided by reason or the masculine part of the soul. By doing so, those noble youths who emulate the tragic hero will become fully transparent or intelligible to their fellow citizens.

However, certain noble youths in liberal modernity, after having entered the ethical, might look to a God who, as love, is higher than the ethical, or beyond the rational moral and social order embodied by their state and its laws. Kierkegaard suggests that if such noble youths can experience the faith of Abraham, they will appreciate a God who, because He is beyond the moral order, can command its violation. For instance, in Abraham's case, that the father shall kill the son, and therefore destroy the nation cryptically hidden within the son. Such commands, Kierkegaard indicates, will induce feelings of great anxiety and dread at being placed outside the universal or the rational moral and social order embodied by their state. Such noble youths, who needless to say will be less than model citizens, will feel themselves as isolated individuals outside the universal. However, they will also be open to a belief in a God who is beyond the natural and temporal order, and thus can violate the universal laws which govern nature and time. Abraham's faith is for this life, and he believes that God will keep his promise and allow Isaac, and the nation within Isaac, to live and die, be and not be, at the same time. This allows Abraham, and therefore those noble youths who emulate him, not only to feel themselves as isolated individuals beyond the universal, but also to act as isolated individuals outside of or against the universal. By feeling and acting as isolated individuals outside of the universal, or rational moral and social order embodied by the modem state and its laws, they will enter into a personal or private relationship with God. Hence, Kierkegaard indicates that they will acquire a higher particularity or individual identity above the universal, or feel a higher passion of the soul beyond the mere passions to which the body gives rise. They will thus unite what Kierkegaard regards as the two parts of the soul, reason, or the masculine part of the soul, and passion, or the feminine part of the soul, with passion understood as higher than reason. However, in elevating love over thought, those noble youths who emulate Abraham and try to found new religions and new nations become completely opaque to other human beings. They cannot communicate their love, or the highest part of their beings, because speech, as Kierkegaard has maintained, cannot express the particular but only the universal; reason cannot grasp passion but only reason or the universal itself.

In presenting Abraham, the greatest of lovers, as the model of human greatness or perfection, Kierkegaard denies Hegel's claim that history can come to an end. For Hegel, the essentially human is reason, that universal characteristic which all human beings share. The essentially human, therefore, can and does become fully manifest in the modern liberal state which recognizes the rationality and therefore equality of all human beings. Because the human being, or the human as such, becomes completely transparent in the modern state, history comes to an end. There is nothing left to do, because everything is known. Kierkegaard, however, in eulogizing Abraham, argues that the essentially human, or the highest part of a human being, is passion not reason, or love not thought. Yet, love is radically particular, and thus individual human beings who feel such love cannot communicate or make this love intelligible to others; they cannot translate their love, or the highest passion of the soul, into the universal. Thus, the highest part of a person is characterized by opacity rather than transparency, and thus can never become completely revealed or known, not even in the modern state. History, therefore, can never come to an end, because the person can never become completely disclosed. For Kierkegaard, as long as love or a higher passion and therefore particularity of the soul is possible, the individual can never become completely socialized or absorbed within the universal, and there will always be a model of human greatness to which noble youths can aspire and possibly make history themselves.

Kierkegaard, in presenting the tragic hero and Abraham as the two choices which the noble youth in modernity face, presents two stark alternatives. Following the path of the tragic hero seems to lead to complete socialization and loss of individual identity. Following the path of Abraham, and therefore following the path of true human greatness, seems to lead to complete isolation and separation from other human beings. According to Kierkegaard, "The true knight of faith is always absolute isolation" (*FT* 79). It seems as if human greatness and human community cannot be combined. In "Problema III," however, Kierkegaard raises the possibility that one can share in community with others without having to relinquish the greatness which Abraham represents. To do so he must look for a type of speech which can express the particular as well as the universal, or the feminine as well as the masculine part of the soul. He therefore must raise the possibility that reason can apprehend passion and not just reason itself. Kierkegaard turns to this problem in "Problema III."

SOCRATES: HUMAN GREATNESS AND HUMAN COMMUNITY

In "Problema III" Kierkegaard asks his third and final question about the story of Abraham: "Was it ethically Defensible for Abraham to Conceal His

Undertaking from Sarah, from Eliezer, and from Isaac?" Again, before answering this question, Kierkegaard gives what he believes is an account of the ethical consistent with an Hegelian understanding of this phenomenon. According to Kierkegaard, the "ethical is the universal; as the universal it is in turn disclosed" (*FT* 82). As a form of disclosure, the ethical is a form of speech or communication. Moreover, as the esthetic individual is hidden, his ethical task is, "to work himself out of his hiddenness and to become disclosed in the universal," or to give over his silence and express himself in a form of speech (*FT* 83). Yet, Kierkegaard again maintains that if Hegel is right and the ethical is the highest form of existence, this means that for Hegel, "there can be no hiddenness rooted in the fact that the single individual as the single individual is higher than the universal" (*FT* 82). Abraham's conduct, therefore, cannot be defended, because he did indeed remain hidden or silent. According to Kierkegaard, "Abraham did not speak, he did not speak to Sarah, or to Eliezer, or to Isaac; he bypassed these three ethical authorities, since for Abraham the ethical had no higher expression than family life" (*FT* 112). Thus, at the beginning of "Problema III," Kierkegaard again makes another contrast between Hegel's two categories of existence and his own understanding of three categories of existence. Hegel's first category of existence is the esthetic, which is associated with hiddenness and thus a form of silence or unintelligibility. Hegel's second and highest category of existence is the ethical, which is associated with a form of disclosure and thus a form of speech or communication. Kierkegaard's third and highest category of existence, however, is faith, which he associates with a higher form of hiddenness of the soul in contrast to the lower form of hiddenness or irrationality of the body. He therefore points to a higher form of silence than esthetic silence, which Kierkegaard identifies as a "divine" silence (*FT* 88).

Kierkegaard, in speaking about the issue of hiddenness and disclosure or speech and silence in "Problema III," is attempting to address the problem of how to combine human greatness with human community, which emerged in the contrast between Abraham and the tragic hero. If the highest part of the soul is passion rather than reason, or love rather than thought, how can it be disclosed or shared with others through the medium of speech, which thus far has always been seen to express the universal? How can one overcome the absolute isolation of Abraham without relinquishing completely the greatness which he represents, and thus retain one's individual identity while becoming or allowing oneself to be part of a larger whole? In order to address this problem, Kierkegaard takes the very unusual step in "Problema III" of identifying a fourth category of existence in addition to the three which he has operated under thus far, the esthetic, the ethical, and the category or paradox of faith. This fourth category of existence is identified by Kierkegaard as "the interesting" (*FT* 83).

The "interesting," according to Kierkegaard, "is a border category between esthetics and ethics" (*FT* 83). Thus, the interesting is beyond the pursuit of the merely physical or sensual pleasures of the body. However, it is indifferent to morality, or questions of right and wrong, or is outside the universal and hence rational moral and social order embodied by the community and its laws. Thus, although the interesting transcends the individuality or particularity derived from the body and the passions to which it gives rise, it is not submersed within the universal. Moreover, when a person has an interesting existence, Kierkegaard says he experiences severe "trouble and pain" (*FT* 83). Thus, the interesting causes one to feel the anxiety and distress of being placed outside the universal or at odds with the ethical. All three characteristics make the category of the interesting similar to the category or paradox of faith. Therefore, although Kierkegaard initially places the interesting between the esthetic and the ethical, it can just as easily be placed, and Kierkegaard encourages the reader to do so as if he or she were looking at it in a mirror, between the ethical and faith.

As a border category, the interesting lies between the particular and the universal, or passion and reason, and therefore between hiddenness and disclosure or silence and speech. As such, this category will allow Kierkegaard to combine human greatness with human community, or privacy and individuation with some form of publicity and socialization.

Socrates, according to Kierkegaard in "Problema III," "was the most interesting man who ever lived, his life the most interesting ever lived" (*FT* 83). Furthermore, inasmuch as Socrates, according to Kierkegaard, had to acquire this interesting life himself without the help of the gods, he, like Abraham, "was not a stranger to trouble and pain" (*FT* 83). The Socratic way of life, therefore, seems to overcome the isolation of Abraham without having to relinquish all of his greatness.

Before his direct treatment of Socrates, Kierkegaard discusses his understanding of Faust. Kierkegaard's interpretation of Faust is the background on which the full import of Socrates' life becomes illuminated. Faust is a doubter, and as a doubter Kierkegaard identifies him as a philosopher (*FT* 6–7). Moreover, Kierkegaard indicates that what Faust doubts is the universal, and thus, like Abraham, Faust becomes, "the single individual who as the single individual stands in absolute relation to the absolute" (*FT* 111). In other words, just as his God places Abraham outside of the universal, now his intellectual propensity to doubt places Faust outside of the universal. Thus, what was an external principle for Abraham—God—now becomes an internal principle or phenomenon of the soul for Faust.[23] However, Kierkegaard indicates that when Faust first doubts the universal, he becomes an "apostate of the spirit who goes the way of the flesh," that is, he falls below the ethical understood as the rational moral and social order embodied by one's political community, into the esthetic, rather than rising above it (*FT* 107–08). Yet,

Faust then turns his doubt away from his society and into himself. According to Kierkegaard, he then also doubts the universal within himself, or that part of the soul which grasps the universal, reason or thought. When Faust becomes self-reflective in this way, "Then he knows that it is spirit that maintains existence, but he also knows that the security and joy in which men live are not grounded in the power of spirit but are easily explained in an unreflected bliss" (*FT* 108). What Kierkegaard suggests is that Faust, in this self-reflective doubt of the universal, learns that the human is essentially soul rather than body, or spirit rather than flesh, and that the core or highest part of the soul is not reason but passion. The highest yearning of the soul is not to grasp the universal, but rather fundamentally to grasp the particular; to love rather than to think. Thus, the individual has a higher end beyond the ethical, and the ethical, therefore, or the rational moral and social order embodied by the community is unstable.

Faust, Kierkegaard maintains, does not speak. He knows that if he expresses his doubt in the universal, or his doubt that reason governs the world, either the internal world of the soul or the external world of the political community, "he throws everything into disorder" or destroys the trust in the ethical which is the basis of human community. Faust, therefore, "remains silent in order to sacrifice himself and save the universal" (*FT* 107, 110).

Socrates, Kierkegaard indicates, was, like Faust, a doubter, and hence a philosopher. As an ancient Greek, Kierkegaard says of Socrates that he, "did know a little about philosophy, assumed to be a task for a whole lifetime, because proficiency in doubting is not acquired in days or weeks" (*FT* 6). For Socrates, therefore, doubt, and hence philosophy, was a way of life, and following this way of life, Socrates "intrepidly denied the certainty of the senses and the certainty of thought" (*FT* 7). Thus, Socrates, like Faust, transcended the body, or the conclusions of the senses, and became self-reflective, doubting the universal within his soul, or the conclusions of the rational faculty. Socrates, like Faust, doubts the universal, or is a single individual who is brought outside universal by his intellectual propensity to doubt. Moreover, in a footnote in "Problema III," Kierkegaard claims that as an "authentic representative of the Greek way of life [. . .] [know yourself]," Socrates, along with Pythagoras, "hinted that, by penetratingly concentrating on oneself, one first and foremost discovers the disposition to evil" (*FT* 100). By discovering the disposition to evil in his self-reflective doubt of the universal, Kierkegaard suggests that Socrates, like Faust, learned that the highest part of the human soul, or the human spirit, is not reason, which grasps the universal or remains satisfied with the ethical, but rather is passion, which grasps at the particular beyond the universal. The human being yearns to love, rather than merely to think, and thus cannot remain satisfied in the ethical. However, there is one crucial difference between Faust and Socrates. Whereas Faust remains silent and thereby sacrifices himself for the universal,

Socrates, in his final moments, according to Kierkegaard, speaks. As a philosopher, therefore, Socrates is not just a doubter but also a speaker, and as such Socrates, unlike Faust, affirms himself, or at least a part of himself, above the universal.

Kierkegaard reveals the significance of Socrates' speech near the end of "Problema III." However, to do so, Kierkegaard draws a distinction between the typical tragic hero that has been presented thus far, of which Agamemnon is a prime example, and a new kind of tragic hero whom he now identifies as an "intellectual tragic hero," of which Socrates, according to Kierkegaard, is an example (*FT* 117). The defining characteristic which distinguishes these two types of tragic heroes, is whether or not they "ought to have last words." This in turn depends on whether or not the tragic hero's life "has intellectual significance, whether his suffering or action is related to spirit" (*FT* 116). Hence, does the tragic hero grasp the universal and therefore understand the soul as essentially mind or reason, or does he grasp the particular beyond the universal, and therefore understand the core or highest part of the soul as passion rather than reason, and thus that he can be a lover as well as a thinker?

Agamemnon, in sacrificing his child for the sake of the nation, makes the movement of infinite resignation whereby he sacrifices the particular to grasp the universal. Thus, his life, according to Kierkegaard, had "no relation to spirit—that is he was not a teacher or a witness of the spirit" (*FT* 116). He should not, therefore, Kierkegaard argues, have last words. Why? Because, "the meaning of his life is an external act, then he has nothing to say, then everything he says is essentially chatter, by which he only diminishes his impact, whereas the tragic conventions enjoin him to complete his task in silence, whether it consists in action or suffering" (*FT* 116). Kierkegaard, therefore, points to the fact that in the very act of sacrificing his child for the nation, Agamemnon enters the ethical and thus becomes disclosed. He already participates in a form of speech by his deed, and therefore any further speaking would be mere idle chatter. Agamemnon's actions speak for themselves. They remain within the teleology of the ethical and are therefore rational, and thus in turn can be rationally apprehended or known by others without further explanation.

However, the life of the intellectual tragic hero such as Socrates, as opposed to the life of Agamemnon, is oriented toward spirit. The intellectual tragic hero, as a doubter of the universal, grasps at the particular which is beyond the universal, and therefore understands the core or highest part of the soul as passion rather than reason. In hence becoming a lover rather than merely a thinker, he moves beyond the ethical and therefore initially beyond what can be rationally apprehended or known by others. His actions, or way of life, do not simply speak for themselves. The intellectual tragic hero, therefore, "ought to have and ought to retain the last word," whereby he "consummates himself in the decisive moment," and "becomes immortal through this last word before he dies" (*FT* 117).

Kierkegaard illustrates his meaning by reference to the trial of Socrates by the Athenian polis, focusing on Socrates' behavior after the death sentence is announced to him. Kierkegaard interprets this scene in the following way:

> His death sentence is announced to him. At that moment he dies [. . .] As a hero Socrates is now required to be calm and collected, but as an intellectual tragic hero he is required to have enough spiritual strength in the final moment to consummate himself. He cannot, as does the ordinary tragic hero, concentrate on self-control in the presence of death, but he must make this movement as quickly as possible so that he is instantly and consciously beyond this struggle and affirms himself. Thus, if Socrates had been silent in the crisis of death, he would have diminished the effect of his life. (*FT* 117)

In the above passage, Kierkegaard suggests that Socrates, in dying at the moment his death sentence is announced to him and remaining calm and collected in the face of his own death, like Agamemnon makes the movement of infinite resignation. Socrates sacrifices the particular for the universal, or sacrifices himself for the sake of the city or the rational moral and social order embodied by the political community and its laws. However, unlike Agamemnon, but like Abraham, Socrates makes one more movement beyond the movement of infinite resignation, the movement of finitude. Like Abraham who, by the power of God, receives Isaac back again after having sacrificed him, Socrates, by his "spiritual strength," "consummates himself" or "affirms himself" above the universal after having sacrificed himself for the universal. In thus grasping the particular beyond the universal, Socrates is moved by a higher passion of the soul in contradistinction to a lower passion of the body, and thus shows himself to be a lover as well as a thinker, that he is both inside and outside the universal at the same time. Yet, Socrates makes this movement of finitude or reveals himself to be a passionate and loving being as well as a rational and thinking being, by speaking after the death sentence is announced to him, or having "the last word," so to speak. Kierkegaard therefore suggests that Socrates had discovered a form of speech which can express the particular as well as the universal, or passion as well as reason. This form of speech, Kierkegaard indicates, is irony.

Socrates' last words, or those by which he affirms himself above the universal, are ironic. Kierkegaard thus says in a footnote to this passage that Socrates' decisive statement, by which he consummates himself as a single individual above the universal, is his, "celebrated response that he is surprised to have been condemned by a majority of three votes" (*FT* 117).[24] According to Kierkegaard, "[Socrates] could not have bantered more ironically with the idle talk in the marketplace or with the foolish comment of an idiot than with the death sentence that condemns him to death" (*FT* 117). Socrates, therefore, by making use of ironic speech, can communicate his passion or make it known to other human beings.[25] He can hence retain his individual identity in love while belonging to a larger whole. Socrates, Kierkegaard suggests, can share in the greatness of Abraham without having to relinquish human community altogether.

Kierkegaard, however, in a very striking reversal at the end of "Problema III," turns Abraham, the father of faith, into an intellectual tragic hero like Socrates, whose life, according to Kierkegaard, "has absolute significance oriented to spirit" (*FT* 117). Abraham, therefore, in order to consummate himself as a single individual above the universal and thereby reveal himself as a lover, must have final words. And indeed, Abraham, at the end of "Problema III" becomes a speaker rather than remaining silent. According to Kierkegaard: "Just one word from [Abraham] has been preserved, his only reply to Isaac, ample evidence that he had not said anything before. Isaac asks Abraham where the lamb is for the burnt offering. 'And Abraham said: God himself will provide the lamb for the burnt offering, my son'" (*FT* 115–16).

Abraham's response to Isaac's question is ironic because, as Kierkegaard says, "it is always irony when I say something and still do not say anything" (*FT* 118). Abraham, in his response to Isaac, says something, because, according to Kierkegaard, if he had said "I know nothing—he would have spoken an untruth," but by saying "God himself will provide the lamb for the burnt offering, my son!" he still does not say anything, because "he is speaking in a strange tongue," and Isaac does not understand him (*FT* 119). Moreover, Kierkegaard claims that this ironic response to Isaac's question expresses the two movements that Abraham makes, that of resignation, whereby he sacrifices Isaac, and that of finitude, whereby he receives Isaac back again. It expresses the former because Abraham believes that God does indeed demand Isaac as the lamb for the burnt offering, and Abraham knows that he himself is willing to sacrifice Isaac as this burnt offering. However, it also reflects the latter, because Abraham believes that, "it is indeed possible that God could do something entirely different," such as provide the ram at the very last moment or restore Isaac back to life after he has been killed (*FT* 119). Kierkegaard therefore suggests that Abraham can make his God, who is love, and his love for this God, known to other human beings who, like Kierkegaard, listen carefully enough, because irony is a form of speech which can express the particular as well as the universal, and thus passion as well as reason. Abraham, like Socrates, can retain his individual identity in love without relinquishing human community altogether. Thus, by transforming Abraham into an ironic speaker, Kierkegaard has transformed *Fear and Trembling*, which began as a eulogy to the greatness of Abraham, into a eulogy to the greatness of Socrates.

NOTES

1. Soren Kierkegaard, *Fear and Trembling: Dialectical Lyric*, Howard V. Hong and Edna H. Hong trans. (Princeton: Princeton University Press), 1983. All subsequent citations will be taken from this edition.

2. Merold Westphal, "Kierkegaard and Hegel," in *The Cambridge Companion to Kierkegaard*, Alastair Hannay and Gordon D. Marion eds. (Cambridge: Cambridge University Press, 1998), 108–10, 121.

3. Also see Edward F. Mooney, "Understanding Abraham: Care, Faith, and the Absurd," in *Kierkegaard's* Fear and Trembling*: Critical Appraisals* (Tuscaloosa, AL: University of Alabama Press, 1981), 100–01, 109.

4. Also see Ronald M. Green, "Developing Fear and Trembling," in *The Cambridge Companion to Kierkegaard*, Alastair Hannay and Gordon D. Marino eds. (Cambridge: Cambridge university Press, 1998), 263–68.

5. See Soren Kierkegaard, *The Sickness Unto Death*, Edward V. Hong and Edna H. Hong eds. and trans. (Princeton: Princeton University Press, 1980), 13.

6. But see Mooney who argues that the knight of faith does not transcend reason but rather transcends selfish for selfless love of the princess. Mooney, "Understanding Abraham," 102, 107–09.

7. But see Mooney, "Understanding Abraham," 109.

8. Also see David Levy, *Eros and Socratic Political Philosophy* (New York: Palgrave MacMillan, 2013): 13; and see Rosalyn Weiss, *Philosophers in the Republic: Plato's Two Paradigms* (Ithaca: Cornell University Press, 2012):14–15.

9. The rational moral duties Kierkegaard has in mind are the abstention from murder, or in Abraham's case the ethical duty of the father to love the son more than himself, as well as obedience to the ethical itself. All political communities, and not just the modern state, demand obedience to their moral codes and hence that the individual subordinate their private good to the common good as such.

10. See Merold Westphal, *Kierkegaard's Critique of Reason and Society* (Macon, GA: Mercer University Press, 1987), 76, and Green, "Developing," 263.

11. Also see Green, "Developing," 267.

12. See Westphal, *Kierkegaard's Critique*, 77, 79.

13. Kierkegaard identifies and briefly describes three tragic heroes: Agamemnon, Jephthah, and Brutus. See Kierkegaard, *Fear and Trembling*, 57–58.

14. Also see Westphal, *Kierkegaard's Critique*, 76.

15. By presenting the tragic hero as able to do what Hegel thinks human beings can only do in the modern state, Kierkegaard criticizes Hegel's teaching that reason only becomes fully manifest at the end of history. Kierkegaard, for instance, claims that if Hegel is right about the ethical, "then no categories are needed other than what Greek philosophy had or what can be deduced from them by consistent thought. Hegel should not have concealed this, for, after all, he had studied Greek philosophy." Kierkegaard, *Fear and Trembling*, 55.

16. See Westphal, *Kierkegaard's Critique*, 80–81.

17. Ibid., 58–59.

18. Ibid., 10, 60, 114.

19. Ibid., 77.

20. Aeschylus, *Agamemnon*, Hugh Lloyd Jones trans. (Berkeley: University of California Press, 1993), 1413–15, 1432.

21. See Sylvia Walsh, "On 'Feminine' and 'Masculine' Forms of Despair," in *Feminist Interpretations of Kierkegaard*, Celine Leon and Sylvia Walsh eds. (University Park: Pennsylvania State University Press, 1997), 207–09; but for an alternative interpretation see Celine Leon, "The No Woman's Land of Kierkegaardian Exceptions," in *Feminist Interpretations of Kierkegaard*, Celine Leon and Sylvia Walsh eds. (University Park: Pennsylvania State University Press, 1997), 149–50, 152–53, 168–69.

22. See *Genesis* 13, 14.

23. But see Westphal, "Kierkegaard and Hegel," 102–04.

24. Also see Plato, *Apology of Socrates*, G.M.A. Grube trans. (Indianapolis: Hackett Publishing Company, 2002), 36a.

25. But see Andrew Cross, "Neither either nor or: The perils of reflexive irony," in *The Cambridge Companion to Kierkegaard*, Alastair Hannay and Gordon D. Mariono eds. (Cambridge: Cambridge University Press, 1998), 128–33.

Chapter Three

Socrates and the God

Kierkegaard's Concept of Irony *and* Philosophical Fragments

In *Fear and Trembling* Kierkegaard argues that Socrates is an intellectual tragic hero whose propensity to doubt places him outside of the universal or the rational moral order of his community, reaching out to a passionate subjectivity like himself beyond the universal. As such, Socrates understands the highest part of the soul as passion rather than reason and thus that he is a lover as well as a thinker. Moreover, Socrates simultaneously affirms his individuality above the universal and discovers a way to communicate his passionate subjectivity to others through the use of ironic speech. Irony, therefore, allows Socrates to share in the greatness of Abraham while maintaining a discursive connection to a larger human whole. Kierkegaard, however, near the end of *Fear and Trembling*, transforms Abraham into an intellectual tragic hero like Socrates by transforming him into an ironic speaker. Kierkegaard, therefore, suggests that his eulogy to the greatness of Abraham, the father of faith, also be understood as a eulogy to Socrates, the first political philosopher or the first to philosophize about the human soul.

Socratic irony is made thematic by Kierkegaard in the *Concept of Irony.* In the "Introduction" to the *Concept of Irony*, Kierkegaard claims that irony was the substance of Socrates' life. Socratic irony in this sense was more than simply a speech act in which Socrates said the opposite of what he meant, but it was also a way of living. Kierkegaard indicates the full import of Socrates' ironic way of life by linking irony to subjectivity and asserting that Socratic irony was, "the historical turning point where subjectivity made its appearance for the first time" (*CI* 264).[1] Moreover, Kierkegaard characterizes irony as a "negative" concept as it is directed against, "the entire given actuality at a certain time under certain conditions" (*CI* 12, 254). Thus, for Kierkegaard, Socrates is, to use Andrew Cross's phrase, the first "existential" ironist to posit his subjectivity or individual identity against the moral and intellectual norms of his age.[2] Kierkegaard argues, therefore, as Hegel does, that by means of his irony Socrates, "destroyed Greek culture" (*CI* 264). Yet, according to Kierkegaard, as we shall see below, Socrates is not destructive of his society because he posits universal ideas above the particulars to which the latter can never live up to, as Hegel maintains. Rather Kierkegaard suggests that Socrates' assertion of his subjectivity remained in "infinite absolute negativity" because, "(i)n irony, the subject is negatively free, since the actuality that is supposed to give the subject content is not there" (*CI* 262). Thus, although he displaces the old, Socrates "does not possess the new," and thereby fails to offer a positive alternative to the established order, the imperfections of which being revealed collapses (*CI* 260–261).

Many scholars have commented on the fact that Kierkegaard, in the *Concept of Irony*, conceives of Socratic irony as a way of living and not simply as a way of speaking; Socrates' verbal irony should be understood as a manifestation of the more fundamental phenomenon of existential irony which calls into question the established moral and intellectual order of one's political community by asserting one's individuality against it.[3] Yet, although there has been much scholarly discussion of the subjectivity and negativity in Socratic irony, there has been less attention to the fact that Kierkegaard presents his analysis as a recovery of the true meaning of Socrates' life after its loss in the many centuries intervening between Socrates' death and the appearance of the *Concept of Irony* in 1841. In this chapter I will investigate the nature of Kierkegaard's restoration of the true meaning of Socratic irony by exploring the question of what, for Kierkegaard, belongs to Socrates and what belongs to Plato in the Platonic dialogues. Moreover, I suggest that in his attempt to disentangle Socrates from Plato, Kierkegaard brings to light an image of Socrates as more than just an individual asserting his subjectivity against the external world, but as the embodiment and object of an *eros* that draws human beings toward a higher individuality rather than the universality of the ideas or forms.[4]

THE DIALOGUE: SOCRATIC QUESTIONS
AND PLATONIC ANSWERS

Kierkegaard begins his analysis of the Platonic dialogues in the *Concept of Irony* by observing that "Plato (felt) himself so inseparably fused with Socrates in the unity of spirit that for him knowledge is co-knowledge with Socrates" (*CI* 30). Plato thus tried to become one with his teacher, unable to love himself or his own thoughts unless he believed they were also the thoughts of Socrates. However, Kierkegaard argues that Plato was unsuccessful in his attempted fusion with Socrates. No matter how loath he was to admit it, Plato added something of his own to the dialogues or conversations that he re-corded between Socrates and his interlocutors. According to Kierkegaard, one can begin to distinguish, "what belongs to Socrates and what belongs to Plato," by following Diogenes Laertius' division between the dramatic di-alogues, such as the *Apology* and the Euthyphro, and the narrated dialogues, such as the *Symposium* and the *Phaedo* (*CI* 30–31). Kierkegaard argues that it is by focusing on the narrated dialogues, and more crucially on how the dialogue or conversation it records arises, that the distinction between Socra-tes and Plato can most clearly be illuminated.

The dialogue arises through the "Socratic art of asking questions" (*CI* 33). Moreover, questions can be asked, according to Kierkegaard, in two ways. The first method, "denotes [. . .] the individual's relation to the subject," the second, "the individual's relation to another individual" (*CI* 34). The purpose of the first method of questioning, Kierkegaard argues, "is [. . .] to free the phenomenon from any finite relation to the individual," and moreover, in this case asking, "becomes identical with answering" (*CI* 34–35). The following scenario may illuminate what Kierkegaard means by his analysis of the first method of questioning. Two individuals see a particular phenomenon or example of beauty in the world, perhaps a beautiful tree. The questioner then asks, "What is this beautiful thing?" or more deeply, "What is beautiful?" The purpose of such questions is to get the one questioned to say what the beautiful thing actually is, and not simply how it appears to him or her as a finite individual. What is the object actually, or what is the separate existence or being of the object free from or independent of how it is perceived by the subject or the finite individual being questioned. Thus the first type of ques-tion aims to reveal the nature of the separate or objective existence of the phenomenon being observed, with the presumption that the questioner al-ready knows the answer that the one questioned is supposed to give. Kierke-gaard calls this first type of questioning the "speculative method," which involves questions that presume and lead to answers (*CI* 36). For the specula-tive questioner, the question "What is beautiful?" should and can be an-swered, and when the answer is given the conversation stops, as we have acquired the "fullness" or "plenitude" of knowledge (*CI* 36).

The purpose and underlying assumption of the second method of ques-tioning is very different from the first. Kierkegaard maintains that a question-er of the second type asks, "without any interest in the answer except to suck out the apparent content by means of the question and thereby to leave an emptiness behind" (*CI* 36). Thus, "inasmuch as every answer contains a possibility of a new question," the purpose of the second type of question is not to find an answer but simply to give rise to another question (*CI* 36).

Kierkegaard calls this second type of questioning the "ironic" method, as it posits questions that are not designed to bring forth answers: it asks questions that do not want or, more fundamentally, do not have stable and final answers, and thus in principle the conversation can continue without end.

Kierkegaard suggests that Socrates is ironic, or practices the second method of questioning, whereas Plato is speculative (*CI* 36, 40–41). Thus, Kierkegaard views the relationship between Socrates and Plato in something like the following manner: Socrates asks, "What is . . .?" and Plato answers, "It is. . ." Plato, unintended by Socrates, answers his teacher's questions. What, therefore, belongs to Plato as opposed to Socrates in the Platonic dialogues? Or what does Plato add to his teacher that was not there originally? Kierkegaard claims that "Socrates' philosophy began with the presupposition that he knew nothing, so it ended with the presupposition that human beings knew nothing at all" (*CI* 37). The irony of Socrates' method, therefore, is that it asks questions the purpose of which are not to find answers, but to show that these questions cannot be answered, that there is no truth or objective reality that the human mind can grasp. The highest knowledge is knowledge of ignorance. Platonic philosophy, by contrast, "began in the immediate unity of thought and being and stayed there" (*CI* 37). If we understand Kierkegaard's use of the terms "thought" and "being" to refer to thinker and that which is, it seems for Kierkegaard that what belongs to Plato rather than Socrates in the Platonic dialogues are the ideas or forms, the things which Are; they are the answers to Socrates' questions. Thus, when Socrates asks, for example, "What is beautiful?" Plato, unintended by Socrates, answers, "It is the idea of the beautiful."[5]

In giving irony to Socrates but speculation to Plato, Kierkegaard presents the former as destructive. For instance, Kierkegaard maintains that Socrates "grasps the pillars that support knowledge and tumbles everything down into the nothingness of ignorance" (*CI* 40). He thus questions his interlocutors' prevailing opinions about the important things such as beauty, goodness and justice, revealing their falsity in the process. However, Socrates does not point his interlocutors toward the truth of such things as beauty, goodness and justice, and even suggests that there is no knowledge concerning these things accessible to human beings.[6] Plato, on the other hand, appears to build something positive on Socrates' destruction. He assures the readers of his dialogues that there are truths or objective realities such as the ideas of the beautiful, the good and the just that exist beyond our false opinions about them and which can be grasped by the human mind. Kierkegaard, however, cautions his readers against unequivocal acceptance of his apparent critique of Socrates and praise of Plato, as he indicates that in answering rather than asking questions, thus desiring to reveal his "wisdom" rather than his ignorance, Plato verges toward sophistry rather than philosophy (*CI* 33).

Socrates' "emptiness" as the Embodiment and Object of Eros

In his analysis of key parts of Plato's *Symposium*, Kierkegaard believes he finds evidence for his interpretation of Socrates' irony and "emptiness" with regard to the ideas, in contrast to Plato's "fullness." Kierkegaard focuses on Socrates' refutation of Agathon to show the destructiveness of Socratic questioning. The fifth speaker after Phaedrus, Pausanias, Eryximachus and Aristophanes to eulogize *eros* as a god, Agathon praises the divine *eros* as beautiful and good (*Sy.* 195a).[7] Socrates is supposed to speak next in praise of *eros* as a god, but instead questions Agathon concerning the understanding of *eros* portrayed in the latter's eulogy. By means of his questions, Socrates establishes that *eros* is love of something that it does not yet possess, namely the beautiful and the good things, and thus *eros* itself is neither beautiful nor good and as such cannot be a god (*Sy.* 200a-201c). In the end, Agathon must agree with Socrates, signifying his awareness that he did not know what *eros* was when he eulogized it; he must acknowledge his ignorance.

Of Socrates' line of questioning concerning Agathon's understanding of *eros*, Kierkegaard remarks, "(l)ove is continually disengaged more and more from the accidental concretion in which it appeared in the previous speeches," such that *eros*, "appears not as love of this or that or for this or that, but as love of something it does not have, that is a desire, a longing" (*CI* 45). Thus, in Socrates' hands, *eros* for Kierkegaard is reduced to, "merely a relation to a something that is not given," denying *eros* any actuality or substance as a thing in itself; it becomes a relation, not a thing (*CI* 46). Kierkegaard argues that Socrates denies substantive existence to every phenomenon under question, and with the example of *eros*, "we see how Socrates does not peel off the husk in order to get at the kernel but scoops out the kernel" (*CI* 45). Kierkegaard appears to suggest, therefore, that by reducing *eros* to a longing or desire separated or abstracted from the object for which it longs or desires, Socrates empties *eros* of any meaning or turns it into nothing.

If Kierkegaard queries with Socrates' refutation of Agathon, can we not query with Kierkegaard's interpretation of this refutation? Socrates, after all, does acknowledge that *eros*, if not beauty and goodness itself, is love of beauty and goodness, thereby not abstracting *eros* entirely from the objects for which it longs. Moreover, after refuting Agathon's understanding of *eros*, and thus showing what *eros* is not, Socrates proceeds to recount what a woman named Diotima taught him concerning what *eros* actually is. According to Socrates, Diotima made him aware that *eros* in the fullest sense is a passion of the soul that opens the philosopher up to the highest form of beauty and draws him toward it through a process, or ladder of love, that moves from particularity to ever greater comprehensiveness and universality (*Sy.* 204a-b). *Eros* first moves the philosopher to love the beautiful body of a

particular person, and then to love of all beautiful bodies. Beyond the body
eros draws the philosopher up to the love of beautiful souls and then the
products of such souls, namely the laws of cities and all of the sciences or
fields of study. *Eros* then reveals or brings the philosopher into the presence
of the highest and most beautiful form of beauty, the idea or being of the
beautiful itself (*Sy.* 210a–212c).

Diotima characterizes the beautiful itself as, "always being and neither
coming to be or perishing, nor increasing nor passing away," and "not beautiful in one respect and ugly in another, nor at one time so, and at another time
not" (*Sy.* 21 1 a). Moreover, it transcends the material and sensible world,
existing "alone by itself and with itself, always being of a single form," and,
"all other things share in it [. . .] in such a way that while it neither becomes
anything more or less . . . the rest do come to be and perish" (*Sy.* 21 lb). The
idea or being of the beautiful itself is, therefore, according to Diotima, eternal, unchanging and immaterial. Moreover, it is the universal characteristic
that all particular and changing examples of beauty in the world share; it is
that quality of beauty that makes the beautiful things what they are and thus
what allows us to think of and name them as beautiful.[8] Grasping or coming
into the presence of this universal Idea, Diotima maintains, allows the philosopher to attain the good, or, "laying hold of the true," to give birth to "true
virtue" (*Sy.* 21 2a).

Socrates, having been taught by Diotima, does indeed seem to connect
eros to the object for which it longs, the idea of the beautiful. Kierkegaard,
however, suggests that Diotima's understanding of *eros* is reflective of Plato's as opposed to Socrates' thought (*CI* 46–47). This is why, Kierkegaard
indicates, Plato does not put this analysis of *eros* and articulation of the idea
of beauty in the *Symposium* in the mouth of Socrates, but rather in the mouth
of this mysterious woman from Mantinea. For Kierkegaard, unlike Hegel,
Socrates is "empty" or without ideas, whereas Plato is "full."

Kierkegaard turns to Alcibiades' speech in the *Symposium* as further
proof that the idea. belongs to Plato rather than to Socrates. Unlike the
previous speakers, having all made *eros* the explicit subject of their praise,
Alcibiades chooses to eulogize the person of Socrates instead (*Sy.* 2 1 4d).
Socrates, therefore, stands in for *eros* in Alcibiades' speech, thus appearing
as the embodiment of *eros* itself. However, Socrates appears not only as its
embodiment but as the object of *eros* as well. For Alcibiades, Socrates, not
the universal idea described by Diotima, is the beautiful for which his *eros*
longs. For instance, Alcibiades asserts that the beauty of Socrates' speeches
are such that, "whenever any one of us hears (Socrates) or another speaking
(Socrates') speeches [. . .] we are thunderstruck and possessed. [. . .]
(W)henever I listen, my heart jumps far more than the Corybants' and tears
pour out under the power of (Socrates') speeches" (*Sy.* 215d–e). The erotic
attraction that Socrates' speeches held for Alcibiades were so powerful that

the latter claims, "I stopped my ears and took off in flight, as if from Sirens, in order that I might not sit here in idleness and grow old beside (Socrates)" (*Sy.* 216a). Alcibiades concludes his speech with the admission that for him, contrary to his initial expectations, Socrates is, "the beloved rather than the lover" (*Sy.* 222b).

Kierkegaard interprets this speech in such a way that for him, as for Alcibiades, Socrates appears as both the embodiment of *eros* and its object at the same time. The interpretation centers on the question of why Alcibiades cannot stop loving Socrates as a particular, concrete individual. Kierkegaard speculates:

> (I)f we ask what it was in Socrates that made such a relation not merely possible but inevitable[. . . .] I have no other answer than it was Socrates' irony. In other words, if their love-relation had involved a rich exchange of ideas . . . then they would, of course, have had the third in which they loved each other—namely the idea, and a relation such as that would never have given rise to such a passionate agitation (*CI* 48).

Kierkegaard's reference to the "third" part of the relationship in which the other two parts—Alcibiades and Socrates—could have loved each other, is a reference to the idea of the beautiful. Thus, Kierkegaard concludes that Alcibiades' erotic attachment to the person of Socrates is evidence that Socrates himself lacks the ideas to which he could have directed Alcibiades' love. In this way, Kierkegaard presents Socrates as the embodiment of the understanding of *eros* that became manifest in the refutation of Agathon. Socrates, as a philosopher, is erotic and therefore longs for something, but empty of ideas, he has no object toward which to direct his erotic longings. Thus, Socrates, like the *eros* that he describes, is for Kierkegaard, "merely a relation to a something that is not given." However, for precisely this reason, Socrates is also the object of *eros*. If Socrates could have helped Alcibiades come to the idea of the beautiful, Alcibiades would have loved the Idea that he and Socrates had arrived at together, and not exclusively Socrates himself. Without the universal idea, Alcibiades is left with only the particular individual to love, which is painful and hard.[9] According to Kierkegaard "(t)he ironist is the vampire who has sucked the blood of the lover and while doing so has fanned him cool, lulled him to sleep, and tormented him with troubled dreams" (*CI* 49).

Kierkegaard's explanation for why Alcibiades remains in love with Socrates also has interesting implications for his understanding of Plato. In positing the ideas, Plato gives himself what Kierkegaard calls the "third" that Alcibiades lacked in his love-relation with Socrates. Plato, it seems, thereby frees himself from the pain, suffering and dependence on Socrates that Alcibiades could not avoid.

PHILOSOPHY AND FAITH

How can Kierkegaard's understanding of the distinction between Socrates and Plato inform our understanding of Socratic greatness and individuality in love? I will explore this question by comparing the contrast between Socrates and Plato in the *Concept of Irony* with the contrast between Socrates and the god in *Philosophical Fragments*. In this latter work Kierkegaard, under the pseudonymous authorship of Johannes Climacus, explores the relationship between philosophy and faith by contrasting Socrates and the god as teachers. Socratic questioning, Kierkegaard initially argues, causes the recollection of truths that were already in the learner. Learning is thus re-affirmation of the self and discarding of the teacher. The god, on the other hand, is a savior who brings knowledge of truth that was beyond the learner. Learning is the discarding of self as one accepts what only the god can give. Scholars such as Jacob Howland argue, however, that for Kierkegaard philosophy and faith are more consistent than at first appears, and that faith may actually be the perfection of Socratic reason rather than its negation. [10]

I argue that Socratic philosophy and religious faith in *Fragments* are both brought together and drawn apart. Kierkegaard initially tries to bring philosophy and faith together by giving a rational account of why an important tenet of Christianity, that the god becomes human, seems necessary. The most significant way, however, in which Kierkegaard brings philosophy and faith together is through his understanding of the condition necessary for grasping the truth brought by the god. This condition involves becoming aware of our ignorance, an awareness that is also brought about by the type of Socratic dialectic described in Plato's *Apology of Socrates*. Yet, Kierkegaard's understanding of philosophy and faith also diverge. For instance, Christianity's beginning point in the existence of god, Kierkegaard suggests, is not open to rational demonstration but rather presupposes faith.

In *Philosophical Fragments* Kierkegaard explores the relation between philosophy and faith, I argue, with two contrasting images of Socrates. When initially drawing philosophy and faith, and hence Socrates and the god, apart, Kierkegaard puts forward an image of Socrates that the *Concept of Irony* would regard as a "Platonic" Socrates. This Socrates, as in the *Meno*, asks "speculative" questions designed to turn the learner inward to recollect ideas or universal truths within themselves that were there but had been forgotten. In this image the philosophic teacher is dispensable and can be cast off as soon as the truth is grasped. Yet, when Kierkegaard begins to draw philosophy and faith, Socrates and the god, together, he puts forward an image of Socrates that the *Concept of Irony* would regard as the ironic or truly "Socratic" Socrates, as it were. This Socrates, as in the *Apology of Socrates*, asks questions not designed to bring forth answers or lead the learner to universal truths within themselves, but rather to show the learner that there are no stable truths human reason can grasp. In this way the "Socratic" Socrates, like Abraham, always keeps the "unknown" as a passionate particularity beyond the universal in front of him, aware that in his search for this passionate or erotic unknown, he is actually searching for an unknown as the missing part of the self.

RECOLLECTION V. REBIRTH

Kierkegaard begins chapter 1 of *Fragments* with the question: "Can the truth be learned?" (*PF* 9).[11] Acknowledging that this is a Socratic question, Kierkegaard thus begins with the problem of the concept of learning raised in the Plato's *Meno*. (*PF* 9). After four failed attempts to define virtue, Socrates reassures Meno, the interlocutor who gives his name to the dialogue, that he still wishes to pursue with him the question of what virtue is. In response, Meno asks, "How will you look for it Socrates, when you do not know at all what it is? How will you aim for something you do not know at all? If you should meet with it, how will you know that this is the thing that you did not know?" (*Meno* 80d). Socrates responds sympathetically by claiming, "I know what you want to say Meno [. . .] that a man cannot search either for what he knows or for what he does not know? He cannot search for what he knows—since he knows it, there is no need to search—nor for what he does not know, for he does not know what to look for" (*Meno,* 80e).

In the above exchange between Meno and Socrates, a number of conditions toward truth are revealed. The first is the condition of the wise, or those who know. Knowers will not search for truth because they already know it and hence learning, for them, is unnecessary. The second condition is that of the ignorant or the non-knowers. Non-knowers are more complex, however, as they can actually take two forms. The first and most apparent form of the non-knower in the exchange above are those who know they are ignorant and hence need to learn the truth, but fear that learning is impossible. For instance, if we do not know what virtue is before we begin, how will we know or have confidence that we have found it in the end. The irony brought out by this condition is that it seems you have to have knowledge of something before you can learn it. The second and less apparent form of the non-knower, implied in the exchange between Socrates and Meno above but made more explicit in Socrates' account of his interrogation of the politicians, poets and artisans in Plato's *Apology of Socrates*, are the ignorant who lack knowledge of their ignorance (*Ap* 21d, 22c, 22d-e). If they remain unaware of their need to learn, they will never begin the search for truth. The goal of Socratic questioning, as described in the *Apology*, is to give the questioned this crucial knowledge of ignorance, a knowledge more likely to arouse hostility toward Socrates rather than love.[12]

The search for truth requires knowledge of ignorance. But even with knowledge of ignorance how can we begin the search if we do not know what we are looking for? As Meno says, "How will you aim for something you do not know at all? If you should meet with it, how will you know that this is the thing that you did not know?" Human learning which seeks to grasp the truth appears to be an impossible activity. To resolve this problem and keep the idea of the search for truth alive, Socrates, Kierkegaard argues, develops the theory of recollection. According to Kierkegaard:

> Socrates thinks through the difficulty by means (of the principle) that all learning and seeking are but recollecting. Thus the ignorant person merely needs to be reminded in order, by himself, to call to mind what he knows. The truth is not introduced into him but was in him. Socrates elaborates on this idea, and in it the Greek pathos is in fact concentrated, since it becomes a demonstration for the immortality of the soul—retrogressively, please note—or a demonstration for the pre-existence of the soul (*Meno* 80d).

Kierkegaard thus refers to Socrates' claim in the *Meno* that, "searching and learning are, as a whole, recollection" (*Meno* 81d). By recollection Socrates means that the learner, when questioned in the right way by the teacher, recollects or brings to the front of their mind truths that were already in them but had been allowed to slip to the back of their mind, as it were. The teacher does not impart or give knowledge, but rather reminds the learner of the knowledge in their souls that they had forgotten was there. Thus, the key to the theory of learning as recollection is that the learner can discover truth through the use of human reason alone.[13] Moreover, Socrates as teacher is a "midwife" who does not himself bring forth truth, but rather by means of his questioning causes the learner to rationally apprehend, or give birth to, as it were, truths that were already gestating within (*PF* 10). Learners do have knowledge of the truth they are looking for before they "learn" it, as it were.

Kierkegaard's account of Socrates as teacher is remarkable in that it appears to reverse the purpose of Socratic questioning put forward by Kierkegaard in the *Concept of Irony*. In the latter, Kierkegaard characterizes Socratic questioning as ironic and leading the learner to knowledge of ignorance. Socrates makes the learner aware that they are a non-knower who thinks they know. In *Philosophical Fragments*, by contrast, Kierkegaard initially characterizes Socratic questioning as leading the learner to knowledge of prior knowledge. Socrates makes the learner aware that they are a knower who mistakenly thinks they don't know; truth is in the learner and can be brought forth through the stimulation of the learner's rational faculty.

In arguing that the theory of recollection resolves not only the problem of learning for Socrates but also serves to demonstrate the immortality of the soul, Kierkegaard moves from reference to the *Meno* to Plato's *Phaedo*. In the *Phaedo*, Socrates argues that when we sense two equal things in this world, such as two equal sticks and stones, if we think about them in the right way we are reminded of the "Equal Itself," or the idea or form of the Equal (*Ph* 74a-b). This same process of recollection holds for all of the ideas or forms; whenever we consider particular manifestations of a thing in this world, such as particular manifestations of beauty, if we contemplate them correctly we are reminded of the universal classification, such as the idea or form beauty itself, that groups the particulars into a class (*Ph* 75d).[14] The knowledge in the soul, therefore, that the learner recollects is knowledge of the universal ideas or forms. But, where did we get this knowledge of the ideas or forms such that we can be reminded of them when considering their particular manifestations? Socrates concludes that the soul must have acquired knowledge of them before we were born, and then "forgot" this knowledge when entering our body upon birth. This shows that the soul, thinking the universal ideas, must exist separate from the body prior to birth, and that the process of recollecting entails overcoming the inhibiting factors of the body after birth (Plato, *Ph* 75c-d, 76c. Also see Plato, *Meno*, 81b-e).

Kierkegaard argues that with the theory of recollection Socrates presents himself not so much as a "teacher" but rather as a "midwife" instead (*PF* 10). As midwife, Socrates helps the learner bring forth or give birth to truths that were already in them, and as such Socrates is the inessential or "accidental" member of the pair (*PF* 11). Kierkegaard thus argues:

> [T]he ultimate idea in all questioning is that the person asked must himself possess the truth and acquire it by himself. The temporal point of departure is a nothing, because in the same moment I discover that I have known the truth from eternity without knowing it, in the same moment that instant is hidden in the eternal, assimilated into it in such a way that I, so to speak, still cannot find it even if I were to look for it, because there is no Here and no There, but only an [. . .] (everywhere and nowhere) (*PF* 13).

Socrates, therefore, once he has helped the learner reveal the knowledge that was concealed in their souls, does not seek credit for having taught anything. Indeed, one of the truths that Socratic questioning attempts to have brought to light is that sentimentality toward the "teacher," or the moment of contact between teacher and learner, is an illusion; who the teacher is and the point in time in which the learner is questioned by them is of no significance to the learner, because truth is in the leaner. This leads Kierkegaard to assert that for Socrates reminding another of the truth within them, "is the highest relation a human being can have to another" (*PF* 10). Reminding is highest because it is impossible for one human being to give to another human being something new or other than themselves that is not already within them. Thus, Kierkegaard says, "In the Socratic view [. . .] self-knowledge is God knowledge" (*PF* 11). The suggestion is that the highest form of human knowledge is knowledge of the self—of the truth within the self and that the truth is within the self—and not knowledge of the other or the higher than the self, such as the god as distinct from the human. Socrates thus posits an equality between himself and other human beings, or between "teacher" and "learner," such that he "does not exclusively and conceitedly cultivate the company of brilliant minds [. . .] but philosophized just as absolutely with whomever he spoke" (*PF* 11).

The alternative to Socrates that Kierkegaard poses is the god. As a teacher, the god, for Kierkegaard, differs from Socrates in four significant ways. First, the god is essential to the learner and hence the moment in time they come into contact will never be forgotten by the learner (*PF* 13). For the learner the god is essential because the leaner does not have the truth within them but rather, as Kierkegaard says, "untruth" (*PF* 13). The second difference is thus that the god is not simply a "midwife" of an idea that was already in the learner, but rather is a teacher in the precise sense in that the god gives or brings truth to the learner. The god teaches the learner what they do not know, and hence one suspects that the truth the god brings is of a different type than that which is within the learner of recollection.

Kierkegaard characterizes the state of untruth, through one's own fault, as sin: "this state—to be untruth and to be that through one's own fault—what can we call it? Let us call it *sin*" (*PF* 15). Sin is thus the human incapacity or lost ability to learn, through their own fault. What does Kierkegaard mean by "through [their] own fault?" He appears to mean that human beings, because of what they are, cannot acquire or regain this ability to learn by their own devices or through human reason alone, but rather require the aid of the god. This leads us to the third way in which the god in Kierkegaard's account differs from Socrates. Not only does the god bring truth to the learner but the god also brings the condition to learn the truth. According to Kierkegaard, "the condition for understanding the truth is like being able to ask about it" (*PF* 14). The condition, therefore, for acquiring the ability to learn is being able to ask, "What is truth?" Since we will only ask "What is truth?" if we learn that we don't know it—that we are in fact in a state of untruth—the condition that the god gives us is knowledge of our own ignorance.

The fourth way in which the god differs from Socrates is that when the god gives the learner the prepatory condition and then the truth itself, the learner is reborn in the sense that they become a person different from what they were before; previously they lacked the truth, but now they have it. Kierkegaard thus suggests that whereas Socrates, as "midwife," causes the learner to give birth in the sense that they recollect and hence bring to light the truth that was already in them, the god, as "savior," causes the learner to be "the one born" in the sense of learning a truth that was other than or outside of the self, becoming thereby a new and different person than they were before. Learning is thus a discarding of the self as one receives the truth and hence the new life that the god and only the god can give.[15]

In this contrast between Socrates and the god as teachers, Kierkegaard initially appears to draw a sharp distinction between philosophy and faith. For the faithful, learning is dependent on the god who must give us the condition for learning the truth and the truth itself. Divine revelation is thus absolutely essential and human reason, due to sin, is severely limited. For the philosophic, learning is a process whereby we recollect, with the help of Socratic questioning, truths already within our souls. Truth, it seems, is accessible to human reason alone and revelation is superfluous.[16] Kierkegaard's apparent implication is that it is difficult to reconcile Socratic rationalism with faith in divine revelation. This conflict is perhaps related to the different concepts of truth utilized by the philosophic and faith paradigms. The philosophic learner recollects universal ideas or truths accessible to human reason alone, whereas the faith learner, by contrast, appears to embrace a passionate subjectivity or particularity beyond the universal. The god, it seems, can be felt but not thought.

THE REASONABLENESS OF CHRISTIANITY?

In chapter 2 of *Fragments*, Kierkegaard attempts to give a rational account of why the god appears as a human being among human beings. Thus, after drawing philosophy and faith apart in chapter 1 he attempts to bring them together in chapter 2 by showing that one of the main beliefs of Christianity, that god becomes human, is reasonable, even while the god is love and hence is felt if not thought.[17] Kierkegaard begins by considering the different motives that Socrates and the god have for teaching. According to Kierkegaard, Socrates teaches or questions his interlocutors because, like his interlocutors, he needs them to recollect the truth within himself. Just as the teacher is for the learner, the learner is the occasion for the teacher's self-understanding (*PF* 24). The difference, therefore, between teacher and learner is minor, as both Socrates and his interlocutors learn through the relationship.

The motive for the god to teach is quite different from that of Socrates. The god is perfectly self-sufficient and thus does not, as Socrates does, need pupils to understand himself, suggesting a radical inequality or lack of reciprocity between the god as teacher and the human leaner; the learner needs god but the god does not need them in return (*PF* 24). Kierkegaard thus speculates:

> What, then, moves him (the god) to make his appearance? He must move himself [. . .] But if he moves himself, then there is of course no need that moves him, as if he himself could not endure silence but was compelled to burst into speech. But if he moves himself and is not moved by need, what moves him then but love, for love does not have the satisfaction of need outside itself but within (*PF* 24).

Kierkegaard, in the above passage, implicitly draws a distinction between human love and divine love. Human love is derived out of deficiency or need and is a feeling of lack, and it is generated by a beloved who appears beautiful and good. Divine love, on the other hand, flowing from a being without need or lack, appears to be derived from something like abundance or overflow—it is love out of sufficiency—and is generated from within the lover, who is god, and not the beloved. The god, in other words, loves for what he is—love, which is the god's essential nature—not for what we or the human beloved are.

The end the god wishes to achieve in becoming a teacher is similar to the motive, namely love, as the god desires that human beings, in gratitude for having received truth from the god, love the god in return. According to Kierkegaard, "The love [of the god] [. . .] must be for the learner, and the goal must be to win him, for only in love is the different made equal, and only in equality or in unity is there understanding" (*PF* 25). Mutual love will overcome the inequality between god and human and thus a secondary motive of the god emerges: to make human beings equal to the god, which means possessing an equality of understanding with the god. Another distinction between human and divine love in Kierkegaard's account therefore emerges. Human love involves sexuality and unhappy love, felt by both lover and beloved, is the failure to unite bodily. Divine love, on the other hand, seeks understanding or intellectual unity—to be of "one mind," as it were, and hence to think the truth together—and unhappy love, felt much more deeply by the god rather than the human—is the failure of intellectual unity. (*PF* 25–26). Notice that the god is portrayed here not simply as love but also mind. As mind the god is infinitely superior to the human being. Given this radical inequality between teacher and learner, it seems that no true and thus happy love is possible between god and man.

Kierkegaard argues that an equality or unity between god and man, if only imperfectly, could be brought about in two ways. The god could elevate human beings to himself, or the god could descend to human beings. The key problem with unity brought about by the ascent of the human learner is that the learner would receive a gift from the god that they could never repay. Yet, for the sake of their happiness the learner would have to be deceived or remain ignorant of this unredeemable debt, or in other words ignore the fact that the inequality between god and human has *not* actually been overcome (*PF* 29). Such ignorance, however, on the part of the learner would make the god unhappy (*PF* 29). The god wants human beings to live in the light of truth, or to be fully aware of their situation, which means being fully aware of their inferiority to the divine. Kierkegaard indicates that the real difficulty is that human beings must attain unity with the god while still understanding that there is a distinction between the human and the divine. The god's task, in other words, involves seemingly irreconcilable contraries: human beings must be united with the god at the same time that they are taught the truth, namely that human beings are radically separate from or inferior to the god. Teaching human beings involves the simultaneous combination of unity and separateness, equality and inequality.

Given the difficulties of unity through the ascent of the learner, Kierkegaard argues that the only possible option is unity through descent of the divine teacher. The god, however, can descend in two ways. The god could descend in his own form as god to human beings. There are, in turn, two problems with this form of divine descent, according to Kierkegaard. First, human beings would glorify the god as the superior when the god wishes to glorify human beings; the god is love and the human is the beloved (*PF* 29). Kierkegaard indicates the second problem when he says, "There was a people who had a good understanding of the divine; this people believed that to see the god was death" (*PF* 30). For the human being, looking on god means death just as, "the shoot of the lily is tender and easily snapped" (*PF* 30). In these passages Kierkegaard suggests that if human beings were to become fully aware of a being so superior to human beings—the god in the form of the god—this would lead human beings to a desire for death; human beings would be overcome by self-loathing and hatred for their inferiority.

The second way the god could descend to avoid producing this self-loathing in human beings for their insufficiency as human, is to descend not in the form of the god but in the form of the human, and the lowliest of human beings at that, the servant and sufferer (*PF* 31). In other words, the god must make himself appear inferior to most other human beings, and at their weakest point, while an infant. Kierkegaard gives the following poetic account of this type of divine descent:

> Look, there he stands—the god. Where? There. Can you not see him? The form of the servant was not something put on. Therefore the god must suffer all things, endure all things, be tried in all things, hunger in the desert, thirst in his agonies, be forsaken in death, absolutely the equal of the lowliest of human beings—look behold the man! (*PF* 32–33)

The story of the god's descent in human form seems to be the story of Christianity, and Kierkegaard, in telling it, attempts to give it a logical grounding.[18] If the god exists he is love, meaning the god loves human beings. The god's love for human beings is a desire for intellectual unity or a meeting of minds between the two, and thus the god must close the gap between the god and the human while still maintaining the distinction between them. Indeed, this appears to be the truth that the god is teaching, that man is not the highest being but rather the god is. The god can only close the gap between the god and the human without destroying the human, by appearing in the form of the human, indeed the lowliest of human beings.

PASSION AND THE PARADOX

In chapter 2, as we have seen, Kierkegaard attempts to give an account of
Christianity that demonstrates its rationality, thereby bringing philosophic
rationalism and faith together. In chapter 3, however, Kierkegaard revises
this account to show that it actually relies on a beginning point that cannot be
rationally proven, namely the existence of the god. To show that the existence of the god is an assumption that is a product of faith rather than reason,
Kierkegaard turns to an analogy with Napoleon and his works. According to
Kierkegaard:

> If one wanted to demonstrate Napoleon's existence from Napoleon's works,
> would it not be most curious, since his existence certainly explains the works
> but the works do not demonstrate *his* existence unless I have already in ad-
> vance interpreted the word "his" in such a way as to have assumed that he
> exists. (*PF* 40–41)

Kierkegaard suggests that if we were to observe the battlefield at Waterloo
and see many dead human beings strewn across it, we would naturally ask
whose doing or work this was. We could answer General Wellington, Tsar
Alexander I, or we could answer General Napoleon. How would we know it
was Napoleon? Because we already know that he exists, who he is, that he
was there on that day and what he did. Kierkegaard's point is that we could
not prove with certainty that Napoleon exists simply by objectively observing his works. On the contrary we would call such works Napoleon's works
based on our prior knowledge that Napoleon exists, who he is, and what he
does or did.

As Napoleon is to his works, so the god is to his. Thus, Kierkegaard
asserts:

> God's works, therefore, only the god can do. Quite correct. But, then, what are
> the god's works? [. . .] Or are the wisdom in nature and the goodness or
> wisdom in Governance right in front of our noses? [. . .] But I still do not
> demonstrate God's existence from such an order of things. (*PF* 42)

Kierkegaard indicates that observing what we believe are the god's works
cannot rationally demonstrate the god's existence. For instance, we observe
the beauty and order in the natural world. We naturally ask, Whose works or
creations are these? Although medieval Christian theologians such as Thomas Aquinas answer that they are the works of the god, others do not. The
ancient Greek philosophers answer that they are no one's works, as the
universe is eternal and not created in time. Modern evolutionary biologists,
on the other hand, answer that they are the products of natural selection. The
indemonstrability of the god's existence from what are believed to be the

god's works brings to light that faith, including Christian faith, has an unphilosophic beginning point.[19]

In chapter 4 Kierkegaard illustrates that not only is Christianity's beginning point rationally indemonstrable, but so is its belief that the god becomes human. Thus, despite his long narrative in chapter 2 that suggests that if the god exists and he is love it is logical that he become human, Kierkegaard now argues that the "paradox"—the eternal (god) becoming historical, and hence born in time becoming flesh—requires the dismissal of reason or the understanding. According to Kierkegaard:

> [W]hen the understanding and the paradox happily encounter each other in the moment, when the understanding steps aside and the paradox gives itself, [. . .] that happy passion [occurs] to which we shall now give a name. We shall call it *faith*. (*PF* 59)

Kierkegaard thus argues that faith—the condition given by the god (the paradox) for grasping the truth that only the god (the paradox) can bring—is "not a knowledge" but a passion (*PF* 62). Again, strictly speaking we feel the presence of the god (in human form) we do not know him.

SOCRATES AND THE UNKNOWN

The rational indemonstrability of the god's existence, for Kierkegaard, results from his notion of what the god is. In chapter 3 the god, for Kierkegaard, signifies the concept of the unknown (*PF* 39). As the unknown, it is that which "thought itself cannot think," and hence is, "the frontier which is continually arrived at [. . .] the absolutely different" (*PF* 37, 44). Kierkegaard says of the unknown, "[d]efined as the absolutely different, it seems to be at the point of being disclosed, but not so, because the understanding cannot even think the absolutely different" (*PF* 45). The concept of the unknown, therefore, points to that which is beyond reason's limits and is thus incomprehensible to it, but which reason nonetheless thinks is there. Since reason thinks the universal, it would appear that the unknown which is absolutely different from reason, to which the name "the god" is given, is a passionate particularity or subjectivity beyond the universal.

Kierkegaard, however, says of Socrates, "[h]e constantly presupposes that the god exists [. . .] If he had been asked why he conducted himself in this manner, he presumably would have explained that he lacked the kind of courage needed to dare to embark on such a voyage of discovery without having behind him the assurance that god exists" (*PF* 44). Pointing to the Socrates of the *Apology* rather than the *Meno*, Kierkegaard seems to suggest that Socrates always kept the unknown, or that which he knew he was ignorant of, before him when he philosophized (*Ap* 21d). Keeping "in mind," as it were, what he did not know, Socrates sought to give his interlocutors the condition that resembled his own; knowledge of ignorance.

Thus, although initially highlighting the gap between Socratic philosophy and the god as the unknown in chapter 3, Kierkegaard also brings them together by pointing to the Socrates of the *Apology*.[20] The point of contact between Socrates and the god in Kierkegaard's account is the condition for learning the truth. Kierkegaard, in chapter 1, describes the condition for learning the truth as "being able to ask about it," and hence as acquiring knowledge that we lack truth and need to seek it. For Kierkegaard, it is the god that gives this condition, which is called "faith" in chapter 4. In the *Apology*, it is Socrates who gives the necessary condition. Of one of his interlocutors Socrates says, "I [. . .] tried to show him that he thought himself wise, but that he was not," and to all those to whom he speaks he tries to show that "human wisdom is worth little or nothing" (*Ap* 21d, 23a).[21] In this way, Socratic questioning or dialectic acts in the same way as the condition, or "faith," given by the god.[22]

In pointing to the Socrates of the *Apology*, moreover, and away from the Socrates of the *Meno* and the theory of recollection, Kierkegaard, in chapter 3, puts forward an image of Socrates that differs from the image initially put forward in chapter 1. The latter was an image of a "Platonic" Socrates that asked speculative questions, causing the learner to turn inward to find universal truths within themselves and away from the god. In chapter 3, however, Kierkegaard now paints an image of an ironic or "Socratic" Socrates, as it were, the purpose of whose questions is not the discovery of truth but rather to show that there are no stable truths human reason can grasp. This "Socratic" Socrates, in other words, gives the learner knowledge of ignorance, and, always keeping the "unknown" before them, they, like Abraham in *Fear and Trembling*, reach out to a passionate subjectivity beyond the universal. Socrates even comes to resemble this passionate subjectivity, giving, like the god, the condition for learning the truth.

Returning to the relation between philosophy and faith, if we consider the purpose of Socratic questioning in the *Apology* in light of the purpose of Socratic questioning in the *Meno*, Kierkegaard's concept of the condition for learning the truth can also be a locus for drawing philosophy and faith apart. In the *Apology*, Socratic questioning, if successful, can lead to knowledge of one's own ignorance and an understanding of the human condition as that of non-knowers who think we know. Socrates, in other words, teaches us that we don't know what we think we know and hence that the truth is not within us. In the *Meno*, on the other hand, Socratic questioning, if successful, can lead to knowledge of one's prior knowledge as we recollect universal truths that are already in us, and we come to understand the human condition as that of knowers who don't know we know. Socrates thus teaches that we all in fact have the truth within us but have forgotten that this is the case.[23]

The positions of the *Apology* and the *Meno* with respect to the purpose of Socratic questioning seem irreconcilable. However, if we consider the two dialogues together, perhaps the teaching is as follows. Socrates first encounters persons who are ignorant but don't know this. His questioning teaches them that they don't know what they think they know, and in acquiring such knowledge of their ignorance Socrates' interlocutors can discard the false opinions about truth that they hold. Yet, this discarding of false opinion would then make possible the second stage of Socratic questioning, illustrated in the *Meno*. In the *Meno* the purpose of Socratic questioning is to allow the interlocutor to recollect the universal truths or ideas that were in their souls but which they had forgotten and had been obscured by the false opinions which they had previously held. Having swept away our false opinions Socratic questioning can help us bring to mind the universal truths we do hold. The crucial difference with Kierkegaard's account is that for Kierkegaard, acquiring knowledge from the god or from Socrates of one's own ignorance or awareness that one is actually in untruth, does not lead one to the recollection of universal truths accessible to human reason alone, but rather opens one up to, or gives one faith in, the possibility of a passionate subjectivity beyond the universal.

Kierkegaard further suggests the assimilation of this ironic, "Socratic" Socrates to the god when he opens chapter 3 by claiming:

> Although Socrates did his very best to gain knowledge of human nature and to know himself [. . .] he nevertheless admitted that the reason he was disinclined to ponder the nature of such creatures as Pegasus and the Gorgons was that he still was not quite clear about himself, whether he [. . .] was a more curious monster than Typhon or a friendlier and simpler being sharing something divine. (*PF* 37)

Kierkegaard suggests that for Socrates to acquire knowledge of what the human being is, and hence self-knowledge, he must acquire knowledge of what the human being is not, or that which is lesser and greater than the human, if only to rule it out. Yet, of the god, or the greater than human, Kierkegaard muses, "But what is the unknown against which the understanding in its paradoxical passion collides and which even disturbs man in his self-knowledge? It is the unknown. But it is not a human being [. . .] or anything else that he knows. Therefore, let us call this unknown the god" (*PF* 39). The nature of god, therefore, as an unknowable, passionate subjectivity beyond the universal that thought desires to think but cannot, ensures that the Socratic quest for knowledge of self and other, or knowledge of the self through knowledge of the whole, will be a task of a lifetime as it can never be fulfilled. Yet, Kierkegaard pairs this desire to know the god for the sake of self-knowledge with the desire to know the erotic part of the self. According to Kierkegaard, "It is the same with the paradox of erotic love. A person lives undisturbed in himself, and then awakens the paradox of self-love as love for another, for one missing" (*PF* 39). Love for another, such as the god, appears to signify or be an image for the love we have for the missing but unknown part of the self.[24] It seems that the god and the story of Christianity as told by Kierkegaard, and other stories which flow from the god, reflects the philosophic condition; faith, as an awareness of the unknown as an erotic, passionate subjectivity beyond the self, manifests an awareness of the unknown as an erotic, passionate subjectivity within the self.

The erotic, as being at the core of both philosophy and faith, is further emphasized by Kierkegaard when he reiterates the necessity of the personal encounter between the god and the religious learner in chapter 4 of *Fragments*, with which I would like to conclude. Here, Kierkegaard contrasts the student of philosophy with the follower of the god come to be in time, or the embodied god, in the following way. According to Kierkegaard, "If I comprehend Spinoza's teaching, then in the moment I comprehend it I am not occupied with Spinoza but with his teaching" (*PF* 62). The teaching of the philosopher, in other words, is accessible to human reason and once grasped by reason the student focuses on the teaching and not the teacher. The truth that the philosopher teaches, to the extent that it can be grasped by reason, stands above any particular human being; it is a universal truth that both teacher and learner can think at the same time, and the learner loves the universal "idea" and not the teacher. The teaching of the embodied god, in contrast, has a very different impact on the learner. Kierkegaard thus argues:

> The object of faith becomes not the *teaching* but the *teacher*, Faith, then, must constantly cling firmly to the teacher. But in order for the teacher to be able to give the condition, he must be the god, and in order to put the learner in possession of it, he must be man. This contradiction is in turn the object of faith and is the paradox, the moment. (*PF* 62)

For Kierkegaard, the truth that the embodied god teaches—I am the god and a human being, the eternal and the historical, the universal and the particular—is not accessible to human reason, but can only be held to by faith. Yet, since it is not accessible to reason, it cannot be separated from the teacher or thought independently by the learner. The embodied god does not give the learner a simple universal to think, but what appears to be a combination of universal and particular or a higher, more absolute particularity beyond the universal which cannot be known in the strict sense but only felt.[25] Thus, like the Alcibiades of the *Symposium* who, for Kierkegaard, cannot direct his love to an idea and hence remains erotically attached to the person of Socrates, the learner is "stuck," as it were, to the embodied god; they cannot move to a universal separate from or beyond the divine teacher.

NOTES

1. Soren Kierkegaard, the *Concept of Irony*, Howard V. Hong and Edna H. Hong trans. and eds. (Princeton: Princeton University Press), 1989. All subsequent citations will be taken from this edition.

2. Andrew Cross, "Neither Either nor or: The perils of reflexive irony," in *The Cambridge Companion to Kierkegaard* (Cambridge: Cambridge University Press, 1998), 126.

3. For example, see Mark Dooley, *The Politics of Exodus: Soren Kierkegaard's Ethics of Responsibility* (New York: Fordham University Press, 2001), 51–53, 55; Cross, "Neither either nor or," 134–38; Sylvianne Agacinski, *Aparte: Conceptions and Death of Soren Kierkegaard*, Kevin Newmark trans. (Tallahassee: Florida State University Press), 55–56, 58–59, 70; John Vignaux Smyth, *A Question of Eros: Irony in Stern, Kierkegaard and Barthes* (Tallahassee: Florida State University Press, 1986), 114; and Harold Sarf, "Reflections on Kierkegaard's Socrates," *Journal of the History of Ideas* 44/2 (1983), 263–65. Also see Brigit Baldwin, "Irony, that 'Little Invisible Personage': A Reading of Kierkegaard's Ghosts," *MLN* 104/5, Comparative Literature (1989), and Peter Fenves, *"Chatter": Language and History in Kierkegaard* (Stanford: Stanford University Press, 1993), 14–18.

4. For a similar view with respect to Kierkegaard's *Philosophical Fragments*, see Jacob Howland, *Kierkegaard and Socrates: A Study in Philosophy and Faith* (New York: Cambridge University Press, 2006), 8, 69.

5. For the importance of Socrates' "What is . . .?" questions, see Strauss who, in contradistinction to Kierkegaard, does not distinguish between Socrates and Plato, and thus appears to give to Socrates both the questions and the answers, or the articulation of the "ideas," in the dialogues. Leo Strauss, *Natural Right and History* (Chicago: University of Chicago Press, 1965), 121–23. Yet, for a view similar to Kierkegaard's in terms of the relation between Socratic questions and Platonic answers, see Hadot, *Ancient Philosophy*, 27.

6. For instance, see Kierkegaard, the *Concept of Irony*, 270; also see Agacinski, *Aparte*, 34, 39, 40, 42, 47–48, 59; and Vignaux Smyth, *A Question of Eros*, 106–08.

7. Plato, *Symposium*, Seth Benardete trans. (Chicago: University of Chicago Press), 1993. All subsequent citations will be taken from this edition.

8. For a similar description of the idea of the beautiful and the ideas generally, see Plato's *Phaedo*, 65e-66a, 100c-e; Plato's *Republic*, 476a-b, 479a; and Mary P. Nichols, *Socrates and the Political Community: An Ancient Debate* (Albany: State University of New York Press, 1988), 112.

9. Hadot argues that in his speech in the *Symposium*, Alcibiades portrays Socrates as the, "Individual dear to Kierkegaard—the individual as unique and unclassifiable personality," and hence in a positive light. Hadot, *Ancient Philosophy*, 30.

10. See Howland, *Kierkegaard and Socrates*, 4–7. For the consistency of philosophy and faith in Kierkegaard's *Fear and Trembling* which also seems to pull them apart, see, for example, Westphal, "Kierkegaard and Hegel," 108–10, 121; and Mooney, "Understanding Abraham," 100–01, 109. Also see Thomas L. Pangle, *Political Philosophy and the God of Abraham* (Baltimore: The Johns Hopkins University Press, 2003), 179–81.

11. Søren Kierkegaard, *Philosophical Fragments, or a Fragment of Philosophy*, Howard V. Hong and Edna H. Hong eds. and trans. (Princeton: Princeton University Press) 1985. All subsequent citations will be taken from this edition.

12. See Plato, *Apology*, 21d, 24b. Also see Plato, *Meno*, 80a–b.

13. See Howland, *Kierkegaard and Socrates*, 28, 30, 46.

14. Also see Paul Stern, *Socratic Rationalism and Political Philosophy: An Interpretation of Plato's Phaedo* (Albany: State University of New York Press, 1993), 197–98; and Ann Ward, "The Immortality of the Soul and the Origin of the Cosmos in Plato's *Phaedo*," in *Matter and Form: From Natural Science to Political Philosophy*, Ann Ward ed. (Lanham, MD: Lexington Books, 2009), 26.

15. See Timothy P. Jackson, "Arminian edification: Kierkegaard on grace and free will," in *The Cambridge Companion to Kierkegaard*, Alastair Hannay and Gordon D. Marion eds. (Cambridge: Cambridge University Press, 1998), 235.

16. See Howland, *Kierkegaard and Socrates*, 30, 46, 48.

17. One can argue that the "core" as opposed to simply one of the main beliefs of Christianity is the "resurrection" of the god after his death on the cross.

18. See Ann Ward, "Socratic Irony and Platonic Ideas? Kierkegaard's 'Critique' of Socrates in *The Concept of Irony*," in *Socrates: Reason or Unreason as the Foundation of European Identity*, Ann Ward ed. (Newcastle: Cambridge Scholars Publishing, 2007), 173–72; and C. Stephen Evans, *Passionate Reason: Making Sense of Kierkegaard's Philosophical Fragments* (Bloomington: Indiana University Press, 1992), 16, 19–21; but see Howland, *Kierkegaard and Socrates*, 29; and David E. Mercer, *Kierkegaard's Living Room: The Relation Between Faith and History in Philosophical Fragments* (Montreal and Kingston: McGill-Queen's University Press, 2001), 63–64, 71.

19. See M. Jamie Ferreira, "Faith and the Kierkegaardian leap," in *The Cambridge Companion to Kierkegaard*, Alastair Hannay and Gordon D. Marion eds. (Cambridge: Cambridge University Press, 1998), 209–10.

20. But see Ferreira, "Faith," 208–09.

21. Howland argues that as Socrates is the occasion for his interlocutors to acquire knowledge of their own ignorance, so the god, understood as distinct from the human but speaking in oracles through the Pythia, is the occasion for Socrates to acquire knowledge of ignorance and is the ultimate warrant for Socratic philosophizing. See Howland, *Kierkegaard and Socrates*, 59, 66–67.

22. But see Jackson, "Arminian edification," 236–37.

23. For a similar relation between the Socrates of Kierkegaard's *Concept of Irony* and the Socrates of *Philosophical Fragments*, see Ward, "Socratic Irony and Platonic Ideas?," 171.

24. But see Howland, *Kierkegaard and Socrates*, 69, 103–04, 113–16, 123, 126–27.

25. Ward, "Socratic Irony and Platonic Ideas?," 173. For a discussion of faith as positing the god and the follower of the god as a higher individuality beyond the universal, see Kierkegaard's *Fear and Trembling*, Howard V. Hong and Edna H. Hong eds. and trans. (Princeton: Princeton University Press, 1983), 55, 73; and Ann Ward, "Abraham, Agnes and Socrates: Love and History in Kierkegaard's *Fear and Trembling*," in *Love and Friendship: Rethinking Politics and Affection in Modern Times*, Eduardo A. Velasquez ed. (Lanham, MD: Lexington Books, 2003), 308–13.

Chapter Four

Socrates and the Search for Individuality

Freedom of Speech and Lifestyle in Mill's On Liberty

In *Fear and Trembling* Kierkegaard presents Socratic philosophy as crucial for human flourishing in liberal modernity, thus critiquing Hegel's call for the end of Socratic dialectic and absorption of the individual into the modern liberal state. Kierkegaard, rather, eulogizes Socrates as an intellectual tragic hero whose propensity to doubt places him outside of the universal or the rational moral order of his community, reaching out to a passionate subjectivity like himself beyond the universal. As such, Kierkegaard suggests that Socrates, the first philosopher of the human soul, understands the highest part of the soul as passion rather than reason and thus that he is a lover as well as a thinker. Moreover, Socrates simultaneously affirms his individuality above the universal and discovers a way to communicate his passionate subjectivity to others through the use of ironic speech. Socratic irony, or his unique way of speaking and asking questions made thematic by Kierkegaard in the *Concept of Irony*, allows Socrates to share in the greatness of Abraham while maintaining a discursive connection to a larger human whole.

Kierkegaard, as he draws Socrates and Abraham together in *Fear and Trembling*, draws Socrates and the god together in *Philosophical Fragments*. He draws the latter two together when he puts forward an image of Socrates that the *Concept of Irony* would regard as the ironic or truly "Socratic" Socrates of the Platonic dialogues. This Socrates, as in the *Apology of Socrates*, asks questions not designed to make the learner aware of universal truths or ideas within themselves, but rather to show the learner that there are no stable truths human reason can grasp. In this way the "Socratic" Socrates, like Abraham, always keeps the "unknown" as a passionate particularity beyond the universal in front of him, aware that in his search for this passionate or erotic subjectivity beyond the self, he is actually searching for a passionate but missing or "unknown" subjectivity within the self. The erotic is at the core of both philosophy and faith.

Like Kierkegaard, the philosopher and politician John Stuart Mill is far from thinking as Hegel does that Socratic philosophy is unnecessary and even unhelpful to the freedom that emerges in liberal modernity. On the contrary, Mill, like Kierkegaard, suggests that it is precisely the Socratic questioning of authoritative opinions that brings into doubt the supposedly rational moral order of one's society, that ensures the flourishing of human freedom in the modern liberal, democratic order.[1]

Mill indicates, therefore, that his understanding of the freedom possible in his time is very different from Hegel's understanding of freedom. For Hegel, freedom means overcoming the individuating constraints of the body and its passions by obeying and thereby internalizing the rational laws of the modern state. In so doing a person sheds "speciality" for universality, becoming one with the whole and free to think rather than simply feel. Mill, on the other hand, in his famous work *On Liberty*, argues that his main concern for the future is not simply the protection of "individual rights" against the tyranny of political rulers by mechanisms such as bills of rights and constitutional checks and balances, but also and to a greater degree the development of "individuality" in the face of what he says is, "a social tyranny more formidable than many kinds of political oppression" (*OL* 8–10, 13–14).[2] Social tyranny, "enslaving the soul itself," is characterized by Mill as, "the tendency of society to impose [. . .] its own ideas and practices as rules of conduct on those who dissent from them," thus preventing any "individual spontaneity" from arising (*OL* 14, 25).

The type of liberty Mill is thus interested in is almost the opposite of that which Hegel envisions; for Mill it is the freedom of each to construct their own unique, individual identity without fear of "the moral coercion of public opinion," or the social stigma that can result when we differ from our fellow citizens, provided we do no harm to others in the process (*OL* 23). Thus, whereas Hegel argues that the individual has the state as their end, Mill believes freedom is defining oneself against it. Moreover, the individuality that liberal freedom makes possible arises, according to Mill, from the erotic "desires" and "impulses" at the core of the soul, the energy from which, properly sublimated, accounts for any intellectual energy the individual may have. Thus, like Kierkegaard, Mill locates human greatness, as it were, not in a universal reason that makes human beings the same, but rather in the passions that make us different and set some unique but indispensable individuals at odds with the reigning social and moral order of their time. Yet, despite these similarities with Kierkegaard, Mill differs from the latter in suggesting a strong distinction between Socratic dialectic that makes possible diversity in thought and lifestyle, and faith. Indeed, Mill is quite critical of religious belief, and Christianity in particular, in a way that Kierkegaard is not.

FREEDOM OF SPEECH

In *On Liberty*, Mill argues that if individuality or the development of idiosyncratic and innovative ways of thinking and acting is to flourish, three freedoms are essential: the freedom of speech, or thought and discussion; the freedom of lifestyle, or tastes and pursuits; and the freedom to associate with like-minded individuals (*OL* 27–28). Beginning with freedom of speech, Mill makes three arguments for why neither government nor society should suppress unorthodox or diverse opinions even if they are believed to be harmful or untrue. First, Mill argues that silenced opinions may be true as we can never be sure of the rightness of prevailing public opinion; the reason of individuals, communities and historical epochs is fallible (*OL* 36). Pointing out in this context that many beliefs and opinions condemned in the past are now accepted as true, Mill offers Socratic teachings as a prime example. Although Socrates is convicted and put to death for impiety and immorality by his fellow Athenians, according to Mill, "we know him as the head and prototype of all subsequent teachers of virtue . . . [as the] acknowledged master of all eminent thinkers who have since lived" (*OL* 49).

The second reason Mill provides for the necessity of near absolute freedom of expression is that, even if opinions are false, the contestation coming from bad or erroneous opinions strengthen, by grounding them in reason, the truthful opinions that we do hold (*OL* 40). Challenges to our most deeply held beliefs, Mill argues, force us to think through why we really believe something is true in the face of such challenges, thus enabling us to give a rational account of our beliefs both to ourselves and others. Contestation, therefore, prevents what may be a true opinion from becoming, "an hereditary creed, [. . .] received passively, not actively [. . .] as if accepting it on trust dispensed with the necessity of realizing it in consciousness" (*OL* 78–79).[3] The third reason for removing all restrictions on speech, according to Mill, is that conflicting opinions may not simply be a struggle between truth and falsehood, but each may represent a partial truth (*OL* 88–89). The example Mill gives is that political life in modern democracies is usually divided between two types of parties: one representing the desire for order and stability the other for progress and reform (*OL* 91–92). According to Mill, both have a claim to truth the expression and exploration of which is beneficial to society.

Mill warns that as scientific knowledge advances and expands, allowing humankind to improve with the progress of history, "the number of doctrines which are no longer disputed or doubted will be constantly on the increase" (*OL* 85). The danger of this "consolidation of opinion" at the end of history is that it may end what Mill perceives as the ongoing conflict of ideas which is ensured when one accepts the three bases for near absolute freedom of speech: silenced opinions may be true, challenges from false opinions strengthen true opinions, and conflicting ideas ensure access to the whole truth. Mill suggests that if the "truth" were fully revealed and universally known in the modern state, this would be problematic because it would undermine the expression of diverse opinions necessary for the development of individuality.[4] In the absence of a natural foundation for the expression of a diversity of opinions, Mill hopes that the, "teachers of mankind [. . .] provide a substitute [or] some contrivance" for it (*OL* 85). The contrivance Mill looks to is Socratic philosophy. According to Mill:

> Socratic dialectics, so magnificently exemplified in the dialogues of Plato, were a contrivance of this description. They were essentially a negative discussion of the great questions of philosophy and life, directed with consummate skill to the purpose of convincing anyone who had merely adopted the commonplaces of received opinion that he did not understand the subject. (*OL* 86)

As the above passage indicates, Mill suggests that his advocacy of the ongoing conflict of ideas necessary for the development of individuality and resting on freedom of speech, is a call for a modern revival of the Socratic dialectical method, especially the Socratic skepticism and questioning of authoritative opinions illustrated in many Platonic dialogues. Mill's Socrates resembles the philosophic World-historical individual that Hegel admires but nonetheless thinks should disappear at the end of history. In contrast, with the danger of the consolidation of opinion looming, Mill believes that Socratic philosophy is even more necessary than it was in the past to protect the freedom made possible in the modern liberal, democratic order.

FREEDOM OF LIFESTYLE

The modern revival of the Socratic dialectical method which ensures the diversity of thought, in turn grounds, Mill argues, the diversity of lifestyles, or what Mill calls "different experiments of living" (*OL* 109). As with the freedom of speech, the only limit that society and government can legitimately impose on the actions of the individual, according to Mill, regards harm to others: "The only part of the conduct of anyone for which he is amenable to society is that which concerns others. In the part which merely concerns himself, his independence is, of right, absolute. Over himself, over his own body and mind, the individual is sovereign" (*OL* 23, 150–51). Thus, a person has an absolute right to err with regard to their own good, and individuals should be free to ruin their own lives if they wish. Why? Mill believes that the pressure to conform "[i]n this age" is so great that, "the mere example of nonconformity, the mere refusal to bend the knee to custom, is itself a service. Precisely because the tyranny of opinion is such as to make eccentricity a reproach, it is desirable, to break through that tyranny, that people should be eccentric" (*OL* 129). Thus, according to Mill, "[a]ll errors which [the individual] is likely to commit against advice and warning are far outweighed by the evil of allowing others to constrain him to what they deem his good" (*OL* 148). Yet, the evil of trying to control individuals for their own good is often not recognized because very few understand the connection between individuality, as it were, and all that is considered "civilized" and "cultured" (*OL* 109).

In defending near absolute freedom of lifestyle, Mill stresses that actions which arouse distaste or disgust are not injurious to others, and therefore should not be limited by social stigma or law. Thus, Mill argues:

> If, for example, a man, through intemperance or extravagance, becomes unable to pay his debts, or, having undertaken the moral responsibility of a family, becomes from the same cause incapable of supporting or educating them, he is deservedly reprobated and might be justly punished; but it is for the breach of duty to his family or creditor, not for the extravagance. (*OL* 156–57)

Mill suggests that although "extravagant" behavior such as excessive drinking, gambling, sexual misconduct or idleness, may arouse disgust, such behaviors are only punishable when they cause direct harm to other individuals such as one's family members or creditors. It is not, therefore, the extravagance that is punishable, socially or legally, but the direct failure of duty to others.[5] Mill further emphasizes that actions that arouse disgust are not in themselves injurious to others in his brief reference to the case of George Branwell. According to Mill, "George Branwell murdered his uncle to get money for his mistress, but if he had done it to set himself up in business, he would equally have been hanged" (*OL* 157). Mill, therefore, believes Branwell should be punished, but not because of the motive for his crime—moral or immoral it would result in the same punishment—but for the direct harm or death that he inflicted on his uncle. In other words, society and law should tolerate his "immoral" lifestyle or unconventional sexual behavior, provided it results in no direct harm to others, just as a moral motive, such as the desire to set oneself up in business, should not lighten the punishment for murder. For Mill, it is only the direct harm to others that is punishable, not the "immoral" or distasteful actions that some may deem harmful only to the one who does them.

Mill elaborates on his argument that all things deemed "immoral" should not therefore be illegal in his disapproval of various sociopolitical movements which seek to prohibit behavior regarded as distasteful but nonetheless harm no one but those engaged in it, believing that such movements are detrimental to human freedom and personal choice. One such sociopolitical movement is the Sabbatarian movement. What is objectionable about Sabbatarians, according to Mill, is not their support of legislation that prohibits work or industry on Sundays, but rather their call for legislation that prohibits entertainment or "amusements," such as train travel, museum going, or even shopping, on Sundays (*OL* 175–76). To the charge that such amusements actually require some people to work on Sundays, such as railway, museum and shop employees, Mill responds that provided such occupations are freely chosen and can be freely resigned, and if need be a holiday on another day of the week is reserved for them, "the pleasure, not to say the useful recreation, of the many is worth the labour of the few" (*OL* 174). Given these conditions are present, the real reason that Sabbatarians seek to prohibit Sunday amusements, Mill claims, is their belief, "that they are religiously wrong" (*OL* 175). Sabbatarians, it seems, wish to legally impose their religious beliefs on others, in order to save the souls of those who, not sharing their beliefs, would pursue such immoral amusements on the Sabbath. Yet, in his concluding remarks on the Sabbatarian movement, Mill argues, "[i]t is a belief that God not only abominates the act of the misbeliever, but will not hold us guiltless if we leave him unmolested" (*OL* 176). Sabbatarians, therefore, are not only trying to save the souls of "immoral" persons against their will, but they believe they need to restrict the freedom of others to save their own as well. Mill's implication is twofold. First, he implies that the law should not take cognizance of such beliefs, thereby suggesting a complete separation of church and state, or religion and politics, as it were, and the embrace of religious pluralism. Second and more deeply, however, he suggests that certain beliefs, such as in a God who punishes persons who engage in various "immoral" behaviors as well as punishing those who tolerate such behaviors in others, is inconsistent with the liberty of speech and lifestyle in a free society.

The temperance movement is another such sociopolitical movement that Mill opposes. Characterizing this movement as a "gross usurpation upon the liberty of private life," Mill argues that in its attempt to prevent behavior which they think is "wrong," namely the consuming of alcohol, the temperance movement goes so far as to call for the legal prohibition of things which "it admits to be innocent," namely the selling of alcohol, as engaging in trade is morally neutral (*OL* 170). Moreover, in calling for the legal ban on the selling of alcohol to ensure that no one actually drinks alcohol, temperance advocates, and indeed almost all "social justice" advocates, claim a "social right" on the part of every individual to force all other individuals to "act in every respect exactly as he ought; that whosoever fails thereof in the smallest particular violates my social right and entitles me to demand from the legislature the removal of the grievance" (*OL* 158). According to Mill, the belief in such "social rights," or that we all have a "vested interest in each other's moral, intellectual, and even physical perfection, to be defined by each claimant according to his own standard," is a concept "so monstrous" as to be "far more dangerous than any single interference with liberty; [. . .] it acknowledges no right to any freedom whatever" (*OL* 173). Of course Mill's opposition to movements such as the temperance and Sabbatarian movements is not simply on the grounds that they seek to restrict individual behavior that is injurious to no one except the person engaging in it, but also because he believes that the offending behavior may not actually be injurious to the idiosyncratic individual who engages in it, but rather is a basis of their potential superiority, as we shall see below.

In defending eccentricity or diversity in lifestyle choices, as it were, Mill is assuming a direct connection between diversity in thought and diversity in action. Thus, Mill asserts, "the same reasons which show that opinion should be free prove also that [the individual] should be allowed, without molestation, to carry [their] opinions into practice at [their] own cost" (*OL* 108). A person with new ideas, Mill suggests, will, if given the liberty to do so, live in new and different ways. Persons of "genius" or "mental superiority," Mill goes so far as to claim, are, "more individual than any other people—less capable, consequently, of fitting themselves, without harmful compression, into any number of the small moulds which society provides in order to save its members the trouble of forming their own character" (*OL* 125). Mill's reasoning is that the strength of one's reason or intellect is derived from the strength of the "energy" that seems to be at the core of one's soul. Thus, Mill argues:

> To say that one person's desires and feelings are stronger and more various than those of another is merely to say that he has more of the raw material of human nature and is therefore capable, perhaps of more evil, but certainly of more good. Strong impulses are but another name for energy. (*OL* 115–16)

For Mill, difference means strength, and energetic individuals with strong impulses are more exemplary of humanity than their peers. By "energy" Mill appears to be referring to the erotic impulses and desires at the core of one's soul, and points toward what Friedrich Nietzsche and Sigmund Freud will later call the process of "sublimation." This is the process by which an individual's erotic energy, with proper education, is rechanneled or transformed into higher mental or intellectual activity. Mill's suggestion seems to be that if we are going to encourage unique or different ideas, we need to allow unique erotic desires or diverse ways of organizing our sexual life to flourish. We should also note that for Mill the source of evil—strong because diverse erotic desires—in human life is also the source of the greatest good. Thus, it seems that the worst criminals had the potential to be the best human beings. The worst criminals push beyond limits or beyond "the pale," as it were, and in this sense are connected to the best because most individual of human beings who introduce new ways of thinking and new ways of living.[6]

Mill defends individuality or eccentricity in thought and action as both useful to progress and as a good in itself. It is useful to progress, according to Mill, because:

> The initiation of wise or noble things comes and must come from individuals; generally at first from some one individual. The honour and glory of the average man is that he is capable of following that initiative; that he can respond internally to wise and noble things, and be led to them with his eyes open. (*OL* 128)

Persons of genius, therefore, although always a "small minority" are, like Hegel's World historical individual, absolutely essential for generating innovative ideas and practices that cause their society to progress to a more advanced stage of history (*OL* 123–24). Yet, although such exceptional individuals, "can only breathe freely in an *atmosphere* of freedom," Mill warns that the, "despotism of custom is everywhere the standing hindrance to human advancement, being in unceasing antagonism to that disposition to aim at something better than customary, which is called [. . .] the spirit of liberty, or that of progress and improvement" (*OL* 135). Originality in thought and lifestyle is thus necessary to improve the human condition, but this becomes more difficult the more society seeks to impose uniform ways of thinking and acting. Mill therefore indicates that great thinkers such as Martin Luther, Rene Descartes, John Locke and others who provided the intellectual foundations for religious, scientific and political revolutions in the past, all required to live in societies that, compared to other societies, provided some measure of toleration of difference or political and social freedom. Such freedom, Mill indicates, needs to continue and even expand if such progressive revolutions are to continue in the future.

Individuality, however, is also for Mill a good or end in itself, necessary for human happiness and well-being independent of its utility to progress. Asserting a radical individualism when he says, "[a]ll that makes existence valuable to anyone depends on the enforcement of restraints upon the actions of other people," Mill defends individuality as he seems to acknowledge contrary to his previous arguments that it is not necessary for sociopolitical progress or change to occur (*OL* 14–15). In the nations of Europe, Mill argues:

> We have discarded the fixed costumes of our forefathers; everyone must still dress like other people, but the fashion may change once or twice a year [. . .] we are eager for improvement in politics, in education, even in morals [. . .] It is not progress we object to; on the contrary, we flatter ourselves that we are the most progressive people who ever lived. It is individuality that we war against. (*OL* 137–38)

Mill thus acknowledges that societies, qua societies, can change and progress without the aid of exceptional and idiosyncratic persons of genius who reach out beyond them, and that it is not progress as such that is the target of society's hostility, as it were, but rather individual divergence from the reigning trend. Yet, if persons simply followed societal norms in how they lived and thought, even if that meant change or evolution, they would be acting like "machines," or "automatons in human form," not human beings exercising choice and freedom (*OL* 114). Moreover, Mill claims that, "[i]t is not by wearing down into uniformity all that is individual in themselves, but by cultivating it and calling it forth, within the limits imposed by the rights and interests of others, that human beings become a noble and beautiful object of contemplation" (*OL* 121). Taken together these arguments suggest that even if Hegel were right that humanity reaches its perfection in the modern liberal state and thus historical change comes to an end, Mill would still defend individuality. The right of the individual to assert their own unique identity, grounded in the near absolute freedom of speech and lifestyle which in turn rests on the revival of Socratic dialectical philosophy, against the assimilating forces of the social whole, is, for Mill, an end in itself worthy of protection.

DEMOCRATIC EQUALITY AND RELIGIOUS FAITH

Defending individuality as both useful for progress and necessary in itself for human happiness and greatness, Mill argues that two conditions must be present if people are to be rendered "unlike one another": "freedom and variety of situations" (*OL* 140). Although Mill believes modern democracies allow for the freedom necessary for the development of individual difference—the "liberal" part of the liberal democratic equation—he is much more circumspect toward the equality of modern democracies that he thinks militates against the second condition, variety of situations (*OL* 142–43). According to Mill, in modern societies:

> The circumstances which surround different classes and Individuals [. . .] are daily becoming more assimilated. Formerly, different ranks, different neighbourhoods, different trades and professions lived in what might be called different worlds [. . .] Comparatively speaking, they now read the same things, listen to the same things, see the same things, go to the same places, have their

> hopes and fears directed to the same objects, have the same rights and liberties, and the same means of asserting them. Great as are the differences of position which remain, they are nothing to those which have ceased. And the assimilation is still proceeding. (*OL* 140–41)

Mill thus indicates that the source of any individuality that may have existed in the past were the substantial inequalities in political, social and economic conditions characteristic of aristocratic societies. With the coming of democracy, however, there occurs not just an expansion of freedom for the individual, but a simultaneous leveling in these areas which militates against such freedom. The French thinker Alexis de Tocqueville coined such leveling or assimilation of lifestyles the "equality of condition," such equality erasing any memory of substantial human differences.[7] The more equal and hence alike people become politically, socially and economically, both Tocqueville and Mill suggest, the less tolerance there will be for individual idiosyncrasy. The democratic person, it seems, has a dangerous logic which assumes that we are equal because we are all the same, and thus anyone desiring to be different must think they are better than the rest. Does the democratic soul envy the exceptional human being and thus seek to suppress them? Mill suggests there is a strong tension between the equality of democracy and the liberty of democracy that allows individuality to arise.

Mill argues that a number of factors are responsible for the rising tide of equality and assimilation of lifestyles in modern democracies. The first are political changes that tend to, "raise the low and to lower the high." (*OL* 141). Mill also cites the extension of education to more segments of the population, improvements in communication technology, and the increase in commerce and manufactures (*OL* 141). Yet, by far the most powerful agent of assimilation is, "the complete establishment, in this and other free countries, of the ascendency of public opinion in the State." (*OL* 142). Mill argues that, "[a]s the various social eminences which enabled persons entrenched on them to disregard the opinion of the multitude" gradually disappear, "the very idea of of resisting the will of the public, when it is positively known that they have a will, disappears more and more from the minds of practical politicians," and any "social support for nonconformity" ceases as well (*OL* 142). From this we can see that Mill's call for the revival of Socratic dialectical philosophy, at first to ensure the diversity ideas in the face of advances in scientific knowledge that threatens to make complete the consolidation of opinion, can also act to ensure the diversity of ideas in the face of advances in the equality of conditions that threatens the dominance of public opinion. Socratic philosophy, requiring the questioning of authoritative opinions which in modern democracy is the "opinion of the multitude," requires its practitioner to question public opinion, just like those entrenched on the "various social eminences" of old did. Mill suggests that the Socratic way of life can act as a substitute in modern liberal democracies for the variety of situations that disappeared with aristocracy.[8]

Mill's defense of individuality in thought and lifestyle would seem to welcome broad tolerance of diverse religious beliefs and practices. This assumption is supported by Mill's opposition, as we have discussed above, to groups such as the Sabbatarians who seek to impose their religious beliefs on others. It is also supported by Mill's selection of the anti-Mormon movement as an example of, "the little account commonly made of human liberty" (*OL* 176). The source of the deep antipathy to Mormonism is its belief in polygamy which, Mill claims, excites "unquenchable animosity when practiced by persons who speak English and profess to be kind of Christians" (*OL* 177). Yet, despite his personal opposition to polygamy because it subordinates women to men, Mill argues that provided Mormon women enter this arrangement voluntarily, Mormons should be allowed to preach their doctrines in England and to practice their beliefs in their own communities (*OL* 177–78). Mill speculates that Mormon women do enter polygamous relationships voluntarily as, given the universal expectation that women "think marriage the one thing needful," it is no surprise that many women "should prefer being one of several wives to not being a wife at all" (*OL* 177–78).

Although Mill's call for tolerance of Mormonism initially seems to suggest his embrace of religious pluralism as a form of diversity of ideas and different experiments in living, upon reflection his arguments actually reveal a strong contempt for this particular expression and practice of faith. Note that Mill believes Mormon preaching should be tolerated only if it is put into practice in their own community in "the midst of a desert [. . .] in a remote corner of the earth" (*OL* 177–78). Moreover, although claiming he is "not aware that any community has a right to force another to be civilized," Mill agrees with its critics' contention that Mormonism is a reversion to "barbarism" in the midst of modern civilization (*OL* 179).

Mill's disapproval of more than simply Mormon expressions of religious belief and practice is revealed in his response to an objection to the first reason he gives for the desirability of near absolute freedom of speech: silenced opinions may be true as we can never assume the rightness or infallibility of our opinions. Mill argues that someone may object: "Are [belief in a God and a future state] the doctrines which you do not deem sufficiently certain to be taken under the protection of law? Is the belief in a God one of the opinions to feel sure of which you hold to be assuming infallibility?" (*OL* 48). Mill answers this hypothetical objector by arguing, "it is not the feeling sure of a doctrine [. . .] which I call an assumption of infallibility. It is the undertaking to decide that question *for others*, without allowing them to hear what can be said on the contrary side" (*OL* 48). The implication that a free, or Socratic, thinker should question the existence of God and the immortality of the soul is furthered by Mill when he refers sympathetically to the treatment of George Jacob Holyoake and Edward Truelove, both of whom were rejected as jury members and insulted in court because, "they honestly declared that they had no theological belief" (*OL* 58–9). In what Mill regards as a greater miscarriage of justice, a foreigner, Baron de Gleichen, was denied redress against a thief because, refusing to profess belief in a God and a future state and thus, "[u]nder pretence that atheists must be liars," was prohibited from giving evidence in court (*OL* 60). For Mill this is tantamount to treating de Gleichen and other atheists as "outlaws, excluded from the protection of the tribunals" (*OL* 59).

The hostility not simply to the core theological doctrine of the existence of God and the immortality of the soul, but to Christian doctrine in particular, becomes apparent in Mill's response to the third reason he gives in his defense of the near absolute freedom of speech: conflicting opinions may not simply be a struggle between truth and falsehood, but each may represent a partial truth. Mill argues that many will strenuously object that, "Christian morality [(is) more than half truths], is the whole truth on the subject, and if anyone teaches a morality which varies from it, he is wholly in error" (*OL* 93–94). The full force of Mill's antipathy to the Judeo-Christian faith and way of life comes to fore in his response to this objection. Mill begins by arguing that the Christian Gospels themselves do not provide a comprehensive ethical doctrine, but rather always refer to a pre-existing morality contained in the "Old Testament" which, for Mill, although elaborate, is "barbarous, and intended only for a barbarous people" (*OL* 94). Beyond the Gospel and its reliance on the Torah, Mill argues that what is called Christian and has been implicitly adopted with slight modification by Protestants is not grounded in the life of Christ or the Apostles, but is of much later origin, "having been gradually built up by the Catholic Church of the first five centuries" (*OL* 95).

Catholic Christianity, according to Mill, has a number of serious defects. In its "horror of sensuality," it idolizes an "asceticism" that has led to the legal suppression of sexual freedom and experimentation (*OL* 96). It encourages its followers to be selfish, holding out "the hope of heaven and the threat of hell" as a self-interested motive for doing our moral duty to others (*OL* 96). It encourages its followers to be servile, inculcating a doctrine of passive obedience and submission to all established authorities who, although "not to be actively obeyed when they command what religion forbids," when they make an alliance with the Church "are not to be resisted, far less rebelled against, for any amount of wrong to ourselves" (*OL* 96). Along with the political servility it inculcates, Catholic Christianity lacks public spirit and depreciates citizenship. According to Mill, "duty to the State" is hardly noticed in "purely Christian ethics," and indeed it is the Koran and not the New Testament that makes just rule and obligations to the public a serious concern (*OL* 97). Even in the morality of private life, Mill asserts, "[w]hatever exists of magnanimity, high-mindedness, personal dignity, even the sense of honour, is derived from the purely human [Greek and Roman], not the religious part of our education" (*OL* 97).

The type of character and way of life that Catholic Christianity produces means that it is a force for "evil" in modern society. Fearing this evil, Mill claims if modern education retains an exclusively religious character, the result will be, "a low, abject, servile type of character which, submit itself as it may to what it deems the Supreme Will, is incapable of rising to or sympathizing in the conception of the Supreme Goodness" (*OL* 99). The "moral regeneration of mankind," therefore, requires the revival of a Socratic dialectic which, resting on the near absolute freedom of speech, questions the truth of Christianity and faith in the existence of God and the immortality of the soul (*OL* 99).[9]

In his attitude toward Socrates Mill shares much with Kierkegaard. Like Kierkegaard and in contrast to Hegel, Mill argues that Socratic dialectic is necessary in liberal modernity to ensure the flourishing of human individuality against the authoritative opinions of society and state. Moreover, like Kierkegaard, Mill locates human greatness in the passions that differentiate human beings from one another, or in what Mill terms the "desires" and "impulses" that provide the "energy" for the superior intellectual activity of the few. Mill, however, differs greatly from Kierkegaard in one respect. Whereas Kierkegaard brings philosophy and faith together, presenting the life of faith as a version of the Socratic life in liberal modernity, Mill draws them drastically apart. Indeed, Mill calls for a revival of Socratic dialectic in order to impugn the life of faith, especially Christian faith.[10]

NOTES

1. Also see Nadia Urbinati, "John Stuart Mill, Romantics' Socrates, and the Public Role of the Intellectual," in *John Stuart Mill: A British Socrates* (Houndmills, UK: Palgrave Macmillan, 2013), 49; and Alan Ryan, "The Philosopher in the Agora," in *John Stuart Mill: A British Socrates* (Houndmills, UK: Palgrave Macmillan, 2013), 154; but see Jonathan Riley who argues that Mill bases his concept of liberty on the Periclean ideal of self-assertion, not the Socratic-Platonic or Christian ideal. Jonathan Riley, "Mill's Greek Ideal of Individuality," in *John Stuart Mill: A British Socrates* (Houndmills, UK: Palgrave Macmillan, 2013), 97–98.

2. John Stuart Mill, *On Liberty* (Boston: Ticknor and Fields), 1863. All subsequent citations will be taken from this edition.

3. Villa goes further, arguing that for Mill a received opinion, simply because it is received and not questioned, becomes for that reason "false." See Villa, *Socratic Citizenship*, 87.

4. Villa denies this, arguing that Mill does not seek diversity of opinion for "its own sake," and goes so far as to argue that Mill wishes to shield liberal opinion concerning the protection and expansion of rights from the "dissolvent rationality" he otherwise advocates. Villa, *Socratic Citizenship*, 89–91.

5. We may wonder if Mill is inadvertently arguing that wealthy persons who can afford an "extravagant" or eccentric lifestyle without falling into debt or alienating and impoverishing their family, should be left alone by society and government to follow their tastes.

6. But see Riley, "Mill's Greek Ideal," 110–12.

7. Alexis de Tocqueville, *Democracy in America*, Henry Reeve trans. (New York: Vintage Classics, 1990), 94.

8. Also see Urbinati, "John Stuart Mill," 54.

9. But see Riley, "Mill's Greek Ideal," 101.

10. Also see Villa, who argues that Mill regarded Christianity as a form of "authoritarianism." Villa, *Socratic Citizenship*, 92, 131.

Chapter Five

Socrates and Dionysus

Nietzsche's Birth of Tragedy

In *On Liberty*, Mill argues that the diversity of opinions faces the danger of disappearance with the progress of science, and the diversity of lifestyles faces the danger of disappearance with the progress of equality and the concomitant loss of the variety of situations or stations in life. In the face of such dangers Mill calls for the revival of a Socratic dialectic that questions the authoritative opinions of the majority in a democracy, thus ensuring an ongoing conflict of ideas that allows for the free development of individuality. Although Mill, in calling for unique and innovative ways of thinking and acting endorses a near absolute freedom of speech and lifestyle, it becomes clear that he does not wish Socratic philosophy to defend various religious ideas and practices as part of the pluralistic conversation within the public sphere, but rather to call them into question, especially Christian ideas and practices.

Mill's critique of Christianity brings him into agreement with philosopher Friedrich Nietzsche. In the "Attempt at Self-Criticism" with which he begins the third edition of *The Birth of Tragedy*, Nietzsche accuses Christianity of a "'[h]atred of the world,' condemnation of the passions," and a "fear of beauty and sensuality," that reveals a *"hostility to life*—a furious, vengeful, antipathy to life itself" (*ASC* 5).[1] To counter Christianity's will to death, as it were, Nietzsche invokes the Greek god Dionysus, apparently calling for a renewal of paganism in our time (*ASC* 5). Moreover, Mill's fear that the equality of democracy poses serious dangers to individual exceptionalism is also shared by Nietzsche. In *Beyond Good and Evil*, Nietzsche argues that the egalitarian morality of democracy brands as pathological the, "highest and strongest drives, when they break out passionately and drive the individ-

ual far above the average and the flats of the herd conscience," therefore
seeking to suppress all true human greatness and virtue in the world (*BGE*
201).[2]

Despite these agreements, however, Mill and Nietzsche diverge in their
attitudes toward Socrates. Whereas Mill celebrates Socratic philosophy as
that which can ground the space for individual diversity in the face of the
tyranny of public opinion and the conformity it seeks to impose, Nietzsche
attacks Socratic philosophy as one of the key problems. Like Christianity,
"Socratism," according to Nietzsche, with its ardor for "logic and logicizing
the world," is at war with the older, Dionysian craving for the ugly, animal
nature of human beings manifested in their bodily passions and desires (*ASC*
4). Moreover, far from being a resource against the leveling tendencies of
democracy, in "The Problem of Socrates" Nietzsche argues that Socratic
dialectic can only be possible with the coming of democratic equality. According to Nietzsche, with Socratic dialectic, "a *noble* taste is thereby defeat-
ed; with dialectic the rabble rises to the top. Before Socrates, dialectical
manners were rejected in good society," and Socrates' irony is, "an expression of revolt [. . .] Of the rabble's *resentment*" (*PS* 14–15).[3] With respect to
the intellectual energy of the select few, whereas Mill argues that this requires the liberal freedom to think and act as you please provided you do not
harm others, Nietzsche believes precisely the opposite. In direct contrast to
Mill, Nietzsche argues that excellence requires the imposition of strict moral
rules, as "[w]hat is essential 'in heaven and on earth' seems to be [. . .] that
there should be *obedience* over a long period of time and in a single direc-
tion" (*BGE* 188).[4]

In their embrace of Socrates and Socratic philosophy, both Kierkegaard
and Mill express a concept of an exceptional individual the core or height of
whose soul is not reason but passion. In *The Birth of Tragedy*, although not
embracing Socrates, Nietzsche does seek to displace the authority of reason,
not simply for the sake of the passions but, going further, to explore the body
itself and its sexual longing for fusion with the unintelligible mass of matter
that it senses living behind the intelligible universe. Thus, coming full circle,
whereas Hegel conceived of freedom as overcoming the individuating constraints of the body and living as pure mind, Nietzsche seeks to get exceptional human beings back in touch with their bodies and hence their sexual
natures. To do so one has to reject the Socratic rationalism which seeks to
master the body and its longings and return to the Dionysian, which we will
explore below. Yet, when Nietzsche concludes *Beyond Good and Evil* with
the invocation of Dionysus, he presents this god, I will argue in the next
chapter, as practising a Socratic dialectic that makes us aware of our ignorance. Thus, just as we discover that Kierkegaard's eulogy to Abraham turns
into a eulogy to Socrates, perhaps Nietzsche's call to revive Dionysus is
actually a call to revive a Socratic form of philosophy.

ART AND THE BODY IN NIETZSCHE'S BIRTH OF TRAGEDY

In *The Birth of Tragedy*, Nietzsche argues that science conquers art, especially the tragic art of the Dionysian poet of ancient Greece. Below we explore Nietzsche's understanding of the unique materialism of Dionysian tragedy by considering his reflections on the origins of tragedy in the tragic chorus. We then turn to the Dionysian confrontation with science or the mind of philosophy. Nietzsche claims that the Greek tragedian embraces life in all its pain by indulging in the *"craving for the ugly"* (*ASC* 4). Embodied by the satyr chorus as the physical image of Dionysus, the "ugly" is understood to be the animal passions of human beings, specifically their sexual drives. Appealing to the natural, primeval self that is suppressed but not extinguished by the knowledge of culture, Dionysian tragedy gets us in touch with our bodies and its deepest longings. Tragedy, strictly speaking, invites us to *feel* the presence of the god and not simply to see or hear him.

Nietzsche argues that tragedy is opposed and eventually destroyed by science.[5] Associated with the "Socratism" of the theoretical man, the response of science, or philosophy, to pain, is quite different from the response of tragedy (*ASC* 1).[6] Craving the "beautiful" rather than the ugly, science and philosophy celebrate the human mind and the rationality of the universe (*ASC* 4). Although Plato, according to Nietzsche, preserves the tragic art form in his dialogues, it is Euripides, another student of Socrates, who destroys the Dionysian entirely. Euripides destroyed Greek tragedy by bringing the *demos* along with their everyday reality on to the stage. By doing so he brought the human individual separated from their god into view. Nietzsche suggests that Euripides celebrated the unadorned individual because only the individual is intelligible or accessible to reason; he wanted art to be comprehended by mind or that it be rationally understood. Euripides was possessed of such a rationalizing drive, Nietzsche claims, because his primary audience was Socrates. It is Socrates, therefore, who is the true opponent of Dionysus.

In suggesting that for Nietzsche Dionysian tragedy attempts to get its audience in touch with their deepest sexual longings, my argument is similar to that of scholars such as Joshua Foa Deinstag. Deinstag argues, "the terrible power of sexuality [is] the center of tragic drama."[7] Moreover, for Deinstag, sexuality, in Nietzsche's view, is more difficult than cruelty to come to terms with not because it is more shameful, as Christianity insists, but because it represents the flux and change that the individuated self is ultimately subject to.[8] Just as the pre-Socratic philosophers viewed the natural universe as in constant, chaotic flux without an underlying order, so the pre-Socratic artist embraced a small part of that nature, human nature, as something constantly in the process of becoming and thus constantly in the process of being destroyed.[9] Sexuality is the chosen symbol of the tragic artist, according to Deinstag, because the "violation of self—simultaneously painful and pleasurable [that it involves] is the simplest and best evidence that our own nature is as unstable and tumultuous as that of the rest of the universe."[10] The human individual, therefore, is characterized by a radical temporality and changeability, made evident by our experience of sexuality.

Giacomo Gambino, like Deinstag, argues that the Greeks found the radical temporality and flux which is the source of human suffering difficult to accept. In response the Greeks sought to create collective identities that could provide some permanence against the relentlessly destructive movement of time, the most refined of these being the *polis*. The *polis*, fostering and protecting individualized existence and hierarchical social structures, stood against a Dionysianism that celebrated the creative, reproductive cycles of nature and opened the Greeks to a primal, undifferentiated being lying beneath and beyond established political identities.

I agree with Deinstag and Gambino that for Nietzsche the Dionysian sought to connect civilized human beings with a primal, sexual nature that exists beneath and beyond particular political identities. Yet, I disagree with their claim that Nietzsche embraced this aspect of tragedy because it fostered democratic tendencies. According to Deinstag, the instability of the self reflected in tragedy, "sanctions a process of identity renovation" that sits uncomfortably with conservative politics.[11] For this reason Deinstag notes that Nietzsche's Dionysian politics has appealed to many radical democratic theorists such as Camus, Arendt, Foucault, and William Connelly.

Gambino argues that the Greek Dionysianism celebrated by Nietzsche reinforces democratic politics in two ways. First, by putting individuals, especially through the music of Dionysus, into contact with their deepest sexual drives, tragedy produced an emotional and even bodily unity between citizens of democratic Athens, more powerful than their contract relations derived from mutual interest.[12] Moreover, in this emotional and physical communalism between citizens, all social and political castes gave way to an ecstatic egalitarianism. Second, although providing the emotional and physical grounding to democratic Athens, the Dionysian, Gambino argues, also connects citizens to the universal human community that exists beyond any particular political regime. As such it opens human beings to "the richness of undifferentiated life beyond established identities," and hence to an appreciation for human plurality essential to democracy as such.[13]

Although Deinstag and Gambino persuasively argue that Nietzsche's analysis of Dionysian tragedy can support a democratic, progressive politics, it seems that Nietzsche himself intends otherwise. Nietzsche argues that Euripides, student of Socrates, destroyed tragedy by attempting to make it rationally intelligible. He did so by moving the democratic individual to the center of the tragic drama. By pointing to Euripides' celebration of democratic individualism as that which caused the Dionysian to disappear, Nietzsche suggests his belief in the aristocratic nature of tragic art.[14]

TRAGEDY AS CHORUS AND THE BODY

Nietzsche turns to the origin of Greek tragedy in section 7 of *The Birth of Tragedy*, and locates the earliest manifestation of tragedy in the tragic chorus.[15] He denies, however, that the chorus has a sociopolitical role, representing the people of democratic Athens viewing the aristocratic scenes on stage (*BT* 7).[16] Rather, the origins of the tragic chorus, according to Nietzsche, are purely religious (*BT* 7). To understand the religious origins of the tragic chorus, and thus of tragedy as such, we must first investigate the role that the chorus played in tragic drama.

The tragic chorus, according to Nietzsche, is a group of actors usually portrayed as satyrs, the half-man half-goat image of the god Dionysus (*ASC* 4, 7). The chorus is usually not on stage itself but at points in the drama will respond to the actors who are or speak directly to the audience in their seats. The chorus is thus both inside the play, when it interacts with the actors on stage, and outside the play when it speaks with the viewing audience. Nietzsche, appearing to accept Schiller's interpretation of the role of the tragic chorus, suggests that the chorus is a "living wall that tragedy constructs around itself in order to preserve its ideal domain and its poetical freedom" (*BT* 7). The chorus, in other words, ensures that the audience views art as art rather than reality. Through the action of the chorus, the audience is reminded that the scene in front of them is fictitious and not real.

In modern drama a similar situation occurs when an actor breaks the dramatic illusion, walks forth and speaks to the audience in his or her own voice. When this happens, we know that we are only watching a play and that the characters, as opposed to the persons, on stage are not real. The chorus, therefore, like the actor in modern drama who breaks the dramatic illusion, divides the world of reality, represented by the audience, from the world of fiction on stage. The chorus separates or divides the audience from the drama in two ways. First, when the chorus speaks to the audience it separates the audience psychically or intellectually; it allows the audience to see art as art or the drama as fiction rather than reality. Second, when the chorus interacts with the actors on stage it separates the audience physically; the audience is excluded from the drama being played out between chorus and actors.

After apparently accepting Schiller's interpretation of the role of the tragic chorus, Nietzsche raises a major problem with it. According to Nietzsche, "*tragedy arose from the tragic chorus*, and was originally only chorus and nothing but chorus" (*BT* 7). In the earliest stages of tragedy, therefore, the chorus *was* the actors or drama on stage, as only the chorus was present. Even the god Dionysus himself, of whom the satyr chorus is an image, was not present or visible, according to Nietzsche, in the oldest period of tragedy (*BT* 66). The significance of the fact that in the earliest form of tragic art only the chorus was present is that the audience is to the chorus what the chorus

will be to the actors on stage in later tragedy. According to Nietzsche, the
logic of this primitive relation is as follows:

> The tragic chorus of the Greeks is forced to recognize real beings in the figures
> on stage. The chorus of the Oceanides really believes that it sees before it the
> Titan Prometheus, and it considers itself as real as the god of the scene. But
> could the highest and purest type of spectator regard Prometheus as bodily
> present and real, as the Oceanides do? Is it characteristic of the ideal spectator
> to run onto the stage and free the god from his torments? (*BT* 7)

Nietzsche suggests that the psychic and physical separation between audience and art maintained by the chorus in later tragedy is absent in earlier
tragedy when the actors on stage have not appeared and all that is present is
audience and chorus. In such a situation, Nietzsche implies, the audience
fails to see art as art or cannot without difficulty distinguish between what is
real and what is fictitious. The psychic separation is absent as art becomes
life and life becomes art when the spectator, running on to the stage to free
their god from torment, becomes part of the scene. Not only is the psychic
separation between audience and drama absent with the sole presence of the
chorus, but the physical separation is absent as well. According to Nietzsche,
"this process of the tragic chorus is the *dramatic* proto-phenomenon: to see
oneself transformed before one's own eyes and to begin to act as if one had
actually entered into another body, another character. This process stands at
the beginning of the origin of drama" (*BT* 8). As the audience experiences
ecstatic union with the chorus, they "surrender their individuality," as Nietzsche characterizes it, and enter into and become another character, namely
their god (*BT* 8). The significance, therefore, of the sole presence of the
chorus at the origin of tragedy is that it encourages the unity of the audience
with art, the spectator with the drama.

The audience of early tragedy could only unite physically with the chorus,
however, or enter into another body, as it were, in a metaphorical way. What
is really happening is that the audience see, or more likely feel, themselves in
the chorus of satyrs. Thus, according to Nietzsche, "we may call the chorus
in its primitive form [. . .] the mirror image in which the Dionysian man
contemplates himself[. . . .] The satyr chorus is [. . .] a vision of the Dionysian mass of spectators" (*BT* 8). Tragedy as chorus, therefore, is self-reflective; the presence of the satyr chorus allows the spectators to become an
object to themselves both individually and collectively. That part of the self
that the audience reflects on or feels when they imagine themselves united
with the satyr chorus is the natural, primeval self that is suppressed but not
extinguished by the culture of civilized life. Nietzsche thus argues:

> The Greek man of culture felt himself nullified in the presence of the satiric
> chorus; [. . .] the gulfs between man and man give way to an overwhelming

> feeling of unity leading back to the very heart of nature. The metaphysical comfort [. . .] that life is at the bottom of things, [. . .] indestructibly powerful and pleasurable [. . .] this comfort appears in incarnate clarity in the chorusof satyrs, a chorus of natural beings who live ineradicably [. . .] behind all civilization and remain eternally the same. (*BT* 7)

Ecstatic union with the satyr chorus and thus with Dionysus himself, Nietzsche indicates, gets the audience in touch with a primeval nature that lies hidden beneath and is constrained by civilized life. Nietzsche gives content to this primeval nature when he describes the satyr as one who "proclaims wisdom from the very heart of nature, a symbol of the sexual omnipotence of nature which the Greeks used to contemplate with reverent wonder" (*BT* 8). As a symbol of the sexual omnipotence of nature in contrast to the "knowledge [. . .] of culture," the uncivilized, natural self that the satyr brings before and gets the audience to feel is their sexual nature. Nietzsche, it seems, associates our experience of tragedy with the arousal of the sexual passions. Thus, whereas civilization appears grounded in rationality and the mind, tragic art, or the Dionysian, appears to arise from nature understood as sexuality and the body. Tragedy, Nietzsche suggests, gets civilized and cultured human beings in touch with their bodies and its deepest longings, longings which have been constrained but not extinguished by the sociopolitical structures within which they live. [17]

After uncovering the Dionysian origins of tragedy Nietzsche turns to the rise of what he calls the "Apollinian" aspect of tragedy. The Apollinian refers to the actual appearance, via an actor, of the god Dionysus on stage with dialogue (*BT* 8, 9, 10). Thus, whereas in the Dionysian aspect of tragedy the god is *felt*, with the Apollinian aspect of tragedy the god is seen and heard (*BT* 8, 9). The Apollinian is the direct visual and verbal presence of the god Dionysus himself, who, Nietzsche claims, was the first character to appear on stage when tragedy developed beyond the tragic chorus (*BT* 10). Moreover, as Dionysus was the first character of Greek tragedy, its sole theme for a long time was the "sufferings of Dionysus" (*BT* 10). Yet, it is reasonable to ask: why is Dionysus suffering? Why is a god in pain? In other words, why is Dionysus associated with tragedy rather than comedy or epic?

THE COSMOS AND THE SUFFERING GOD

Nietzsche argues that Dionysus is the suffering god because the existence of an intelligible universe means that he is a dismembered god. Nietzsche gives clarity to what is meant by Dionysus as the dismembered god when he says:

> In truth [. . .] the hero [of tragedy] is the suffering Dionysus of the Mysteries, the god experiencing in himself the agonies of individuation, of whom won-

derful myths tell that as a boy he was torn to pieces by the Titans and now is worshipped in this state as Zagreus. Thus it is intimated that this dismemberment, the properly Dionysian *suffering*, is like a transformation into air, water, earth, and fire, that we are therefore to regard the state of individuation as the origin and primal cause of all suffering, as something objectionable in itself. From the smile of this Dionysus sprang the Olympian gods, from his tears sprang man. In this existence as a dismembered god, Dionysus possesses the dual nature of a cruel, barbarized demon and a mild, gentle ruler. (*BT* 10)

Nietzsche indicates that according to Greek myth the process of the god's dismemberment—the separation or individuation of his being—is the creation of the universe. The image that Nietzsche draws is that before the cosmos comes into being, what exists is unified, undifferentiated matter.[18] This undifferentiated mass of matter can be understood as the god Dionysus in his original condition. The god, however, is then torn to pieces or individuated, as Nietzsche would say, which can be understood as the process of creation. After this creative action, there exist a number of particular and therefore intelligible beings in the cosmos, such as Olympian gods, human beings, animals, plants, and the elements earth, air, fire and water. All of these particular pieces of the whole are actually the body of Dionysus separated or alienated from itself. The suffering of Dionysus, therefore, is caused by his dismemberment, which is also the Greek story of the coming into being and continuation of an intelligible universe.

In relation to sexuality—the presence of the suffering Dionysus in us— our bodily longing for union with another body seems to reflect our longing for the original unity of matter that we believe existed before our world came into being. Thus, in our ecstatic desire to free Dionysus from his sufferings we reflect our deepest wish to return into an undifferentiated material being prior to the creation of the cosmos.[19] The ultimate but unachievable aim of sexuality, therefore, seems to be the fusing of our material existence into matter as a whole, such that all matter or body would come together in a way that would destroy our world. In this sense sexuality desires to transcend all limits or boundaries, not just moral boundaries but also physical-factual boundaries. Thus, Nietzsche says of the rapture of the Dionysian state that it is the "annihilation of ordinary bounds and limits of existence" (*BT* 7). Sexuality, in other words, points to the desire to crush together all individuated matter, such that human is fused into human, humanity into trees, trees into earth, and so on, until we are left without form and shape in one undifferentiated mass of material. In such a state the cosmos would be unintelligible as matter can only be grasped by thought when it is individuated into particular shapes. Intrinsic in our experience of sexuality, therefore, is pain at and perhaps even rebellion against an intelligible universe. One might be tempted to say that for Nietzsche, sexuality is inherently anti-rational.[20]

Nietzsche claims that the suffering Dionysus was for a long time the only character beyond the satyr chorus to be represented on the tragic stage. Yet, in later periods, other tragic heroes make their way into the tragic drama. Characterized by Nietzsche as simply particular "masks" of the god Dionysus himself, these tragic heroes are complex mixes of the Apollinian and Dionysian (*BT* 10). They are Apollinian in the sense that they are visual and verbal images of Dionysus, but Dionysian in the sense that behind this visual and verbal mask they are the god himself. The two most celebrated of these heroes in Greek tragedy are Aeschylus' Prometheus and Sophocles' Oedipus. Nietzsche first addresses the character of Oedipus. In his brief analysis, Nietzsche focuses on the murder of his father, marriage to his mother, and Oedipus' ability to solve the riddle of the Sphinx, namely: what is a human being. Nietzsche then considers what "the mysterious triad of these fateful deeds tell us" (*BT* 9). According to Nietzsche:

> With the riddle-solving and mother-marrying Oedipus in mind, we must immediately interpret this to mean that where prophetic and magical powers have broken the spell of present and future, the rigid law of individuation, and the real magic of nature, some enormously unnatural event—such as incest—must have occurred earlier, as a cause. (*BT* 9)

Incest, according to Nietzsche, is an unnatural violation of the law of individuation. Oedipus violates this law by attempting, albeit unintentionally, to become his own creator; by sleeping with his mother he acts as if he were his own father, or if parent and child could become one. Yet, as Nietzsche argues, such violation of nature actually gives Oedipus knowledge of nature. Oedipus discovers that after the cosmos comes into being he cannot, as he attempted, become one with his father; after creation individuation is our second nature, as it were. Oedipus is specifically a Dionysian hero because, through sexuality, he tries to become his own father and thus overcome the physical individuation between parent and child. Through such Dionysian rebellion Oedipus learns that what can be called the tragedy of the body—its intrinsic longing for the destruction of individuation—is the tragedy of life— the body is that which is most particular and thus, paradoxically, that which most prevents the overcoming of individuation.[21]

After discussing Sophocles' Oedipus, Nietzsche provides a brief analysis of Aeschylus' Prometheus. According to Greek myth Prometheus was a Titan who, at war with the Olympian gods, steals fire from them and gives it to human beings. For this he is punished by Zeus who chains him to the side of a mountain and has a vulture perpetually eat out his liver. Fire is such a prized possession, according to Nietzsche, because it carries with it the power of the sun, which is the source of life, and the destructive power of lightning, which can end life (*BT* 9). In having the power to give life and take it away, fire represents the power of the gods and is also symbolic of sexuality. Sex is creative of life and, in its longing for the fusion of matter such that individuation would be overcome, sex actually longs for the destruction of life. Prometheus is Dionysian when he steals fire from the gods and gives it to human beings because in doing so he tries to overcome the individuation or separation between god and man.[22] By putting the power to give and take life into the hands of human beings, Prometheus allows them to become gods, as it were.

Nietzsche claims that the Greeks viewed Prometheus' attempt to close the gap between god and human as a sacrilege (*BT* 9). Greek tragedy, however, under the hand of Aeschylus, dignifies this sin and provides what Nietzsche characterizes as a "justification of human evil" (*BT* 9). In other words, such prideful rebellion against the gods is indeed sinful but also necessary for human elevation and civilization. Moreover, Nietzsche contrasts this Greek tragic myth of Prometheus with the biblical story of the fall in the Garden of Eden. Both are stories of rebellion against god or the attempt to close the gap between the human and the divine. Yet, as Nietzsche points out, Greek tragedy views this sin "as something masculine" whereas the Bible understands it "as feminine" (*BT* 9). Thus, for the Greeks, "the original sacrilege is committed by a man," for the Hebrews "the original sin [is committed] by a woman" (*BT* 9). Nietzsche suggests that in placing the original sin against god in a man the Greeks sought to justify it, whereas in placing it in a woman the Hebrews meant to condemn it. Nietzsche indicates that he prefers the Greek Promethean myth because, unlike the biblical story, it glorifies the human rather than the divine.[23] In doing so it glorifies sexuality and the desire to overcome individuation, especially between god and human, at its core.

THE MIND AND THE DEATH OF TRAGEDY

Greek tragedy, Nietzsche argues, is confronted by and eventually dies under the glare of the "Socratism [. . .] of the theoretical man" (*ASC* 1). Two such Socratic theorists who were especially important to the demise of Dionysian tragedy, according to Nietzsche, are Plato and Euripides. Plato, Nietzsche suggests, transforms the undifferentiated matter of Dionysus that can only be felt into the universal idea that can only be thought (*BT* 10). Yet, Plato does preserve the tragic art form in his dialogues, but nonetheless makes this art form subservient to Socratic rationalism (*BT* 14). It is Euripides, according to Nietzsche, another student of Socrates and himself a tragic poet, who destroys the Dionysian entirely.

Nietzsche provides both a "provisional" explanation and a final explanation for how Euripides, paradoxically, caused Greek tragedy to disappear.

The problem with Euripides from the point of view of tragedy is that he "brought the *spectator* onto the stage" (*BT* 11). Provisionally, Nietzsche means that Euripides portrayed the *demos*, or the common "everyday man" with his common, everyday reality, in the drama. Thus, according to Nietzsche, "civic mediocrity, on which Euripides built all his political hopes, was now given a voice, while heretofore the demigod in tragedy and the drunken satyr [. . .] had determined the language" (*BT* 11). Moreover, Nietzsche argues, "if the entire populace now philosophized, managed land and goods, and conducted lawsuits with unheard-of circumspection, [Euripides] deserved the credit, for this was the result of the wisdom he had inculcated in the people" (*BT* 11). Euripides, therefore, does not merely portray democratic man on the tragic stage, but also produces an art form that grounds the democratic regime that serves his interests. In other words, Euripides is too democratic. It seems that for Nietzsche Dionysian tragedy is aristocratic, representing not democratic man but noble human beings and the god himself as tragic heroes.

Euripides' democratic tendencies as that which causes the death of tragedy is only Nietzsche's provisional explanation, however. Penetrating more deeply into Euripides' tendencies Nietzsche claims that he finds two additional "spectators" brought on to the tragic stage. The first of these is "Euripides himself, [but] Euripides as *thinker*, not as poet" (*BT* 11). An indication of what Nietzsche means by this can be gleaned from his statement that "somebody, I do not know who, has claimed that all individuals, taken as individuals, are comic and hence untragic—from which it can be inferred that the Greeks [prior to Euripides] simply *could* not suffer individuals on the tragic stage" (*BT* 10). Nietzsche, therefore, suggests that Euripides, using his mind as a thinker rather than his passions as a poet, puts the human individual as an individuated piece of matter which speaks, or has *logos*, on the stage. This individual is separated and completely cut off from its god, which is the universal, undifferentiated matter that the tragic hero was a "mask" for in earlier tragedy. In Euripides, the tragic hero represents an individual human being as an individual human being, and nothing deeper. In other words, the Euripidean tragic hero is completely Apollinian without any connection to the Dionysian from which the Apollinian originated. Euripides puts this solely Apollinian individual at the center of his drama because, according to Nietzsche:

> [Euripides] [. . .] often [. . .] felt as if he had to bring to life for drama the beginning of the essay of Anaxagoras: "In the beginning all things were mixed together; then came the understanding and created order." [. . .] As long as the sole ruler and disposer of the universe, the *nous*, remained excluded from artistic activity, things were all mixed together in a primeval chaos: this is what Euripides must have thought (*BT* 12).

Euripides, in other words, insisted that art be rationally comprehended by *nous*, or the intellect. He therefore celebrates the unadorned individual because only the individual is accessible to reason. Since there are no "ideas" in the Platonic sense for Euripides, it is only individuated pieces of matter with *logos* which can be thought or comprehended. The undifferentiated matter of Dionysus, or the primeval chaos that exists prior to *nous*, is completely unintelligible; it cannot be thought but only felt through sexuality.

Euripides desired to make tragedy completely rational, thereby causing its demise, because Socrates was the second of the two additional spectators brought to bear on the tragic stage by Euripides (*BT* 12). Nietzsche suggests that Euripides wanted Socrates' approval for his dramatic productions. Yet, since his "logical nature" was excessively overdeveloped, Socrates, according to Nietzsche, held that "to be good everything must be conscious" (*BT* 12, 13). Arising out of the sense of the primeval, material chaos that existed prior to creation, "Old Tragedy" could not be comprehended completely by reason and thus was not esteemed by the abnormally logical Socrates (*BT* 12). In order to win the approval of this master logician Euripides had to initiate a new art form in his tragedies, an art form, Nietzsche claims, in which "to be beautiful everything must be conscious" (*BT* 12). Since the body and its deepest longings cannot be brought fully into rational consciousness, that aspect of the older tragedy, the Dionysian aspect, had to disappear. Moreover, because it is as a follower of Socrates that Euripides banishes the Dionysian from the tragic stage, Nietzsche claims that is Socrates who is the true opponent of Dionysus.[24]

In identifying Socrates as the driving force behind the fall of Greek tragedy, Nietzsche provides his readers with an account of the confrontation between the Dionysian and the Apollinian. The Apollinian begins as the visual and verbal appearance of the god Dionysus, either as the god himself or instantiated through a tragic hero as one of his masks. Thus, the dialogue of tragedy, or its Apollinian aspect, was originally meant to give voice to the body or speech to sexuality and the undifferentiated material being that was felt to lie behind it. Reason, Nietzsche suggests, arises from matter.[25] The problem with Socrates and the theoretical-scientific individuals who take Socrates' lead, is that for these individuals reason and speech become separated from their origins in the body and the sexual, and eventually turn against both (*BT* 15). Such separation between mind and body, speech and sexuality pushes Euripides, according to Nietzsche, to "separate this original and all powerful Dionysian element from tragedy, and to reconstruct tragedy purely on the basis of an un-Dionysian art, morality and world view" (*BT* 12). The about-face, as it were, that reason does against the body and all things material is, according to Nietzsche, not only the downfall of Old Tragedy, but at the origin of Western civilization and forms the spirit of Christianity (*ASC* 5).

NOTES

1. Friedrich Nietzsche, "Attempt at Self-Criticism," in *The Birth of Tragedy and the Case of Wagner*. Walter Kaufmann trans. (New York: Vintage), 1967. All citations refer to aphorisms and will be taken from this edition. But see Bertram, who speculates that Nietzsche is actually a Christian because he most loves and identifies with those he is most insulting toward. Ernst Bertram, *Nietzsche's Attempt at a Mythology*, Robert E. Norton trans. (Urbana: University of Illinois Press, 2009), 262. Also, see Zuckert, *Postmodern Platos*, 27.

2. Friedrich Nietzsche, *Beyond Good and Evil: Prelude to a Philosophy of the Future*, Walter Kaufmann trans. (New York: Vintage), 1966. All citations refer to aphorisms and will be taken from this edition.

3. Friedrich Nietzsche, "The Problem of Socrates," in *Twilight of the Idols*, Richard Polt trans. (Indianapolis: Hackett Publishing company), 1997. All citations refer to page numbers and will be taken from this edition.

4. Also see Bertram, *Nietzsche*, 283. But see Villa who makes the opposite argument. Villa, *Socratic Citizenship*, 134.

5. Laurence Lampert denies that as an advocate of art Nietzsche was an enemy of science. Rather, Lampert argues that Nietzsche's philosophy advances a science that breaks with both the Platonic science of the transcendence of nature and the Baconian science of the mastery of nature to embrace what Lampert calls a science of "pure immanentism or naturalism" that is wholly consistent with the naturalistic worldview of contemporary biology and ecology. See Laurence Lampert, *Nietzsche and Modern Times: a Study of Bacon, Descartes, and Nietzsche* (New Haven: Yale University Press, 1993) 10–11.

6. Also see Aristide Tessitore, "Nietzsche or Socrates: Reflections on European Identity," in *Socrates: Reason or Unreason as the Foundation of European Identity*, Ann Ward ed., (Newcastle, UK: Cambridge Scholars Publishing, 2007), 196–97; but see Laurence Lampert, *Leo Strauss and Nietzsche*, (Chicago: University of Chicago Press, 1996), 127.

7. Joshua Foa Deinstag, "Tragedy, Pessimism, Nietzsche," *New Literary History* 35/1 (2004): 92.

8. Ibid., 92.

9. Ibid., 87.

10. Ibid., 92.

11. Ibid., 94–95.

12. Giacomo Gambino, "Nietzsche and the Greeks: Identity, Politics and Tragedy," *Polity* 28/4 (1996): 428; also see Ingrid Makus, "Nietzsche's criticism of Socratic Reason and the Problem of Identity," in *Socrates: Reason or Unreason as the Foundation of European Identity*, Ann Ward ed. (Newcastle, UK: Cambridge Scholars Publishing, 2007), 215–16.

13. Gambino, "Nietzsche and the Greeks," 416.

14. See also Ofelia Schutte, "Nietzsche's Politics," in *Feminist Interpretations of Friedrich Nietzsche*, Kelly Oliver and Marilyn Pearsall eds. (University Park: Pennsylvania State University Press, 1998), 286–87.

15. For an alternative approach that denies that the origins or the primitive manifestations of the Dionysian captures its essence, see Benjamin Bennett, "Nietzsche's Idea of Myth: The Birth of Tragedy from the Spirit of Eighteenth-Century Aesthetics," *PMLA* 94(3) (1979): 420–22.

16. Friedrich Nietzsche, *The Birth of Tragedy and the Case of Wagner*. Walter Kaufmann trans. (New York: Vintage), 1967. All citations refer to aphorisms and will be taken from this edition.

17. Oliver and Pearsall suggest that Nietzsche's embrace of the Dionysian and the importance he places on the body open promising avenues for feminist philosophy. See Kelly Oliver and Marilyn Pearsall, "Why Feminists Read Nietzsche," in *Feminist Interpretations of Friedrich Nietzsche*, Kelly Oliver and Marilyn Pearsall eds. (University Park: Pennsylvania State University Press, 1998), 3–4. For a similar argument that suggests that Nietzsche's Dionysus is feminine, see Kofman, "Baubo: Theological Perversion and Fetishism," in *Feminist Interpretations of Friedrich Nietzsche*, Kelly Oliver and Marilyn Pearsall eds. (University Park: Pennsylvania State University Press, 1998), 44–46. For alternative readings that question Nietzsche's

value for feminist philosophy and egalitarian politics, see Ofelia Schutte, "Nietzsche's Politics," in *Feminist Interpretations of Friedrich Nietzsche*, Kelly Oliver and Marilyn Pearsall eds. (University Park: Pennsylvania State University Press, 1998), 294–99, and Owen, "Nietzsche's Squandered Seductions: Feminism, the Body, and the Politics of Genealogy," in *Feminist Interpretations of Friedrich Nietzsche*, Kelly Oliver and Marilyn Pearsall eds. (University Park: Pennsylvania State University Press, 1998), 321–23.

18. This interpretation is consistent with Nietzsche's attempt to return to a Presocratic worldview. For instance, Milesian philosophers sought to discover the one material cause at the origin of or lying behind all being in the cosmos.

19. See Lampert for Nietzsche's embrace of the earth and the transience of all being, Lampert (1993), *Nietzsche and Modern Times: a Study of Bacon, Descartes, and Nietzsche* 11–12. Also see Makus, (2007), "Nietzsche's Criticism of Socratic Reason and the Problem of Identity," 212.

20. One could also say that sexuality is "beyond good and evil," as it were.

21. But see Jeffrey Church, "Two concepts of culture in the early Nietzsche," *European Journal of Political Theory* 10/3 (2011): 334–35.

22. But see Church, "Two concepts of culture," 334–36.

23. Also see Lampert, *Leo Strauss and Nietzsche*, 119, 126.

24. Also see Bertram, *Nietzsche*, 264; Makus, "Nietzsche's Criticism of Socratic Reason," 212; and Zuckert, *Postmodern Platos*, 11–12, 14.

25. For a similar argument, see Zuckert, *Postmodern Platos*, 19.

Chapter Six

Socrates, Democracy, and the End of Man

Nietzsche's Beyond Good and Evil

In *The Birth of Tragedy*, Nietzsche associates Socrates with a democratic drive to disembodied reason that destroys the aristocratic art form of Dionysian tragedy. The Dionysian element in ancient tragedy, according to Nietzsche, evokes the body and sexuality as longing for cosmic unity. In *Beyond Good and Evil* he associates Socratic rationalism with a type of dialectical questioning that undermines aristocratic moral codes, those codes that seek to conceal and contain the Dionysian that underlies them. With "the craftiness of the plebeian," and hence valuing rationality more highly than instinct, Socrates, according to Nietzsche, demanded of human beings that they, "evaluate and act in accordance with reasons, with a 'why?'" (*BGE* 190–91). Thus, siding with reason, Socrates spent his whole life, "laugh[ing] at the awkward incapacity of noble Athenians who, like all noble men, were men of instinct and never could give sufficient information about the reasons for their actions" (*BGE* 191). Socrates, however, also secretly laughed at himself, discovering, upon self-examination, his "same difficulty and incapacity" in giving a rational account for his actions (*BGE* 191). Thus, like Nietzsche who views the body and sexuality as the hidden source of rationality and science, Socrates, Nietzsche argues in *Beyond Good and Evil*, discovers the non-rational, instinctive grounding for all rational moral judgments. Socrates, therefore, is not just destructive but also dishonest. The "real falseness of that great ironic," according to Nietzsche, is that while still asking his interlocutors for reasons for their actions, Socrates had, "at bottom, [. . .] seen through the irrational element in moral judgements" (*BGE* 191).[1]

Nietzsche indicates that in seeking, dishonestly, a rational foundation for moral action, Socrates sought knowledge of good and evil (*BGE* 202).[2] Not finding it, however, Nietzsche claims that, "one knows in Europe [today] what Socrates thought he did not know and what that famous old serpent once promised to teach—[. . .] one 'knows' what is good and evil" (*BGE* 202). Modern European morality, therefore, arises from and understands itself as the heir and perfection of Socratic philosophy. Yet, Nietzsche claims, "Morality in Europe today is herd animal morality" (*BGE* 202). The Socratic inheritance, therefore, is the morality of the herd, or what Nietzsche calls the "democratic movement" (*BGE* 202). Lumped together, as it were, with Socratism—or the pursuit of what is good and what is evil—in the democratic movement are Judaism, Christianity, liberalism, anarchism and socialism (*BGE* 195, 202). The problem with the democratic movement, as suggested above, is that it is leading to the "overall degeneration of man [. . .] [the] diminution of man into the perfect herd animal" (*BGE* 203).

Despite Nietzsche's apparent hostility to democracy, Jeffrey Church, in *Nietzsche's Culture of Humanity: Beyond Aristocracy and Democracy in the Early Period*, argues that Nietzsche is a classical liberal thinker in his commitment to the equality and freedom of all human beings, adhering to the democratic claim that all persons are capable of excellence.[3] Yet, according to Church, Nietzsche in his writings sought to move out of the political realm and form a new community, the community of culture.[4] It is within this new community of culture that Nietzsche wishes to mediate between "aristocracy" and "democracy." Culture, for Nietzsche, is simultaneously "aristocratic," encompassing the highest human achievements in art, literature and philosophy, and "democratic," encompassing the local and particular, or the customs and habits of a particular city or group. Church adds to this insightful analysis with his theory of the exemplary individual in Nietzsche's thought; it is exemplary individuals who mediate between aristocracy and democracy, cosmopolitanism and nationalism, in the community of culture. One of the most important of these exemplary individuals, Church argues, is Socrates.[5]

My analysis of *Beyond Good and Evil* builds on yet also offers an alternative to Church's investigation Nietzsche's thought. Like Church, I argue that Nietzsche seeks to restore the beauty of individuality in our democratic age, and although apparently critical, ultimately regards Socrates as an exemplar of such individuality. However, unlike Church, I do not remove Nietzsche's thought from the realm of politics into an alternative realm of culture, but rather situate it in a political frame. As a result, my reading of Nietzsche understands him as much more critical of the liberal democratic politics of our age. Thus, I argue that for Nietzsche, genius, as Church refers to it, does not arise out of liberal freedom, as Mill argues, but rather the feeling of constraint or unfreedom that comes when one is bound to conform to strict moral codes. Moreover, although I argue that Nietzsche believes democratic morality may have irreversibly altered the human condition thus making impossible the attempt to overturn democratic political structures, I also argue that the nobility conjured out of a democratic age is, for Nietzsche, a pale shadow, or falling off, as it were, of the nobility as such that human beings are capable of.

SOCRATES AND THE "SCIENCE OF MORALS"

Returning to the democratic movement's search for good and evil, we can begin to understand why for Nietzsche it spells the diminution of man if we look to the beginning of Part Five of *Beyond Good and Evil* and the discussion of modern Europe's philosophic search for the "science of morals" (*BGE* 186). The problem with the "science of morals," according to Nietzsche, is that by means of it, "our philosophers [. . .] want [. . .] to supply a rational foundation for morality—and every philosopher so far has believed that he has provided such a foundation. Morality, itself, however, [is] accepted as a 'given'" (*BGE* 186). Modern Europeans, therefore, following in Socrates' footsteps without apparently being aware of Socrates' dishonesty, in seeking a rational foundation for morality assume that there is one morality which is right and as such universally accessible to human reason alone. This is problematic, however, because, being "poorly informed and not even very curious about different peoples, times, and past ages," our philosophers, Nietzsche argues, do not understand that all moral codes are relative to the various historical epochs and cultural contexts in which they occur (*BGE* 186). To understand the relativity of morals and thus gain a perspective outside of one's own moral horizon, Nietzsche suggests, one must study the different moralities in history. This is precisely what our philosophers do not do, and thus what they are really doing, according to Nietzsche, is not providing a rational foundation for a universal morality as such, but rather simply providing a justification for the particular democratic morality of our time (*BGE* 186).

Another problem with the science of morals, Nietzsche argues, in addition to its unwitting defense of a particular morality in its attempt to provide a rational foundation for a universal morality, is the content, or the conception of the good, of the particular democratic morality it is defending. According to Nietzsche, quoting Schopenhauer, "the fundamental proposition on whose contents all moral philosophers are really agreed—[hurt no one; rather, help all as much as you can]—that is really the proposition for which all moralists endeavor to find a rational foundation" (*BGE* 186). Yet, such a proposition, according to Nietzsche, is "insipidly false and sentimental;" the directive to hurt no one but rather help all cannot be true or reasonable, as it were, "in a world whose essence is will to power" (*BGE* 186). An irrational passion—the will to power—and not reason is the source of all morality and human actions. Nietzsche suggests that the truly reasonable would be to see reason's limits and acknowledge the will to power as the essence of life. Nietzsche indicates what he means by the will to power when he says:

> One is much more of an artist than one knows. . . . In an animated conversation I often see the face of the person with whom I am talking so clearly and so subtly determined in accordance with the thought he expresses, or that I believe has been produced in him, that this degree of clarity far surpasses my powers of vision: so the subtle shades of the play of the muscles and the expression of the eyes must have been made up by me. Probably the person made an altogether different face, or none at all (*BGE* 192).

Nietzsche suggests that as an "artist," he makes the facial expressions and internal thoughts of his interlocutor into what he wants them to be rather than what they really are. Nietzsche takes what is other and makes it his own, or what is foreign and makes it familiar (*BGE* 192). Thus, we are "liars" or "artists' in our interactions with others because we try to control their actions and thoughts and make them conform to our wishes. The will to power, therefore, is the desire to possess and control others, thereby recreating the world to our own liking. This irrational desire to possess and control others by turning them into what we want them to be, thereby denying them what Mill would regard as their own unique, individual identity, is at the root of all morality including, Nietzsche argues, the morality of harm none but help all. Taking the example of charity, the virtue that would most seem to exemplify this latter morality, Nietzsche claims the charitable, giving expression to their will to power, first turn the poor into the "deserving" poor—for instance distributing food stamps which can be exchanged only for healthy choices as opposed to money that could be used to purchase alcohol or cigarettes—and then expect and enjoy their recipients' affection and obedience (*BGE* 194). The charitable become angry if they are "crossed" in their desire to help—for instance to deny entry to refugees that the charitable are eager to provide with hospitality and generosity—because, Nietzsche suggests, one thereby denies them the feeling of power over the help that they seek (*BGE* 194). Nietzsche's point is that all moral claims are really expressions of a desire to control the thoughts and actions of others in order to turn them into what the moral claimant wants them to be. But what do moral claimants, especially those who are the creators of new moral codes, most want others to be? Referring to Kant, Nietzsche says, "Some moralists want to vent their power and creative whims on humanity; some others, perhaps including Kant, suggest with their morality: 'What deserves respect in me is that I can obey— and you ought not be different from me'" (*BGE* 187). What we want others most to be, therefore, is a copy of ourselves, understanding ourselves as obedient and thus self-controlled. Recreating the world to our own liking is recreating the world in our own image, an image of self-control, thereby denying others, as Mill would say, a unique identity different from oneself.

THE NECESSITY OF MORALITY AND THE
ATTACK ON PERMISSIVENESS

Nietzsche seems highly critical on morality: there is no one right moral code universally accessible to human reason, and all moral codes are at bottom an expression of the will to power, the desire to dominate and control, first ourselves, and then others. Thus, according to Nietzsche, "[e]very morality is, as opposed to [letting go], a bit of tyranny against 'nature'; also against 'reason'" (*BGE* 188). Also, as we saw in *The Birth of Tragedy*, the Dionysian art form encourages and is an expression of the sexual omnipotence of nature that is concealed by the rules of culture. Yet, unlike Mill who cautions against society imposing moral judgments on its members, Nietzsche believes that the imposition of tyrannical moral rules is essential for human flourishing and greatness. According to Nietzsche:

> The curious fact is that all there is or has been on earth of freedom, subtlety, boldness, dance, and masterly sureness, whether in thought itself or in government, or in rhetoric and persuasion, in the arts just as in ethics, has developed only owing to the "tyranny of such capricious laws"; and in all seriousness, the probability is by no means small that precisely this is "nature" and "natural"— and not that [letting go]. (*BGE* 188)

Contrary to Kierkegaard, who argues in *Fear and Trembling* that greatness such as Abraham's requires the teleological suspension of the ethical, Nietzsche indicates that all human greatness—artistic creativity, virtue, rational thought, spirituality—has been the result of the tyranny of capricious moral or ethical rules.[6] Thus, for Nietzsche, it is a mistake to view, as Mill does, laws and restrictions as stifling to human nature. The true understanding of human nature is not letting go, but rather "self-mortification," as it were. Human beings need and respond to laws and commands. Such capricious or tyrannical laws that restrain the passions produce human excellence because they educate "the spirit," or "purify" and "sharpen" the powerful drives of the soul (*BGE* 188, 189). The Christian attack on sexuality, according to Nietzsche, is an example of the European spirit's education to greatness in times past. Arguing that in the "Christian period" the sex drive "sublimated" itself into love, Nietzsche indicates that spiritual education requires sublimation, a concept not named but also pointed to by Mill (*BGE* 189). By sublimation, Nietzsche indicates the rechanneling of the "drives," or raw passions of the soul, toward higher things such as the beautiful and the good represented in theology, philosophy, poetry and art, or the products of higher culture more generally. In this way Christian constraints, Nietzsche suggests, caused the erotic drive to be rechanneled or transformed from the body to the soul; from a bodily desire for the body of the beloved to a passion in the soul for the soul of the beloved. After sublimation spirit desires to be loved in return by the beloved, lifting *eros* above the body to something more beautiful.

As the Apollonian arises out of the Dionysian, it seems that from sublimation we derive the soul, or something more spiritual, out of the body. Nietzsche's concern, however, is that sublimation will only occur if the drives are restrained by rules that prevent their immediate satisfaction. The more capricious or tyrannical because irrational those rules are felt, the better. If the drives are not restrained, they will dissipate; sex will never turn into love, anger will never turn into poetry or philosophy. Human greatness thus disappears and the individual slips into mediocrity. Moreover, Nietzsche argues that what may be true for individual human beings is even truer for nations and peoples. The strength, life, vitality and greatness of peoples and nations, Nietzsche argues, requires the closing of their horizon's to other ways of life, what Nietzsche characterizes as a narrowing of perspective or even "stupidity" (*BGE* 188). Thus, it seems that for Nietzsche open, cosmopolitan and culturally tolerant societies are weak and incapable of greatness. Healthy and strong peoples, in contrast, close off other ways of life and understandings of right and wrong, adhering strictly to their own moral order. Members of the society "throw themselves into it entirely," as it were, living out what can be regarded as an extreme patriotism or nationalism.[7] Great peoples are great, Nietzsche suggests, not because they allow each to think and live as they choose as Mill would believe, but rather because of their discipline, commitment and devotion to their own moral code.

HERD MORALITY AND THE ATTACK ON THOSE WHO COMMAND

Nietzsche, as we have seen, argues that all moral codes are, "a bit of tyranny against 'nature'; also against 'reason'." Yet, Nietzsche asserts that such tyranny is, "in itself [. . .] no objection, as long as we do not have some other morality which permits us to decree that every kind of tyranny and unreason is impermissible" (*BGE* 188). What is this other morality that condemns tyranny and unreason? Nietzsche turns to the Torah, arguing that:

> The Jews have brought off that miraculous feat of an inversion of values [. . .]: their prophets have fused "rich," "godless," "evil," "violent," and "sensual" into one and were the first to use the word "world" as an opprobrium. This inversion of values (which includes using the word "poor" as synonymous

with "holy" and "friend") constitutes the significance of the Jewish people:
they mark the beginning of the slave rebellion in morals. (*BGE* 195)

The "slave rebellion in morals," for Nietzsche, is a moral movement that praises the humble and the low, and hence the tyrannized over, and condemns the proud and the strong, and hence those who do the tyrannizing. In contrast to Kierkegaard who presents Abraham, the father of faith, as the exemplar of human greatness, Nietzsche locates the origin and most powerful expression of this slave rebellion in the Torah. Moreover, Nietzsche associates this slave morality not only with Judaism, but also with Socratism, Christianity, liberalism, anarchism and socialism, lumping all together under one rubric: the "democratic movement" or the movement of the "herd," those whose "instinct of obedience is inherited best, and at the expense of the art of commanding" (*BGE* 199, 202).

Nietzsche argues that the aim of those who obey is to give those who command a bad conscience such that the latter, styling themselves as mere executors of higher commands such as those that come from the people's will, the constitution, the ancestors and even from God, believe they obey too (*BGE* 199). Nietzsche calls this, "the moral hypocrisy of those commanding" (*BGE* 199). Such hypocrisy results from the herd's branding of all those drives "dangerous to equality," that "when they break out passionately and drive the individual far above the average and the flats of the herd conscience, wreck the self-confidence of the community [. . .] as if its spine is snapped," as pathological or "evil" (*BGE* 201). These dangerous drives feared by the herd include pride, arrogance, independence, cruelty, hardness, the "lust for rule," and even a "powerful reason" (*BGE* 201). Those traits that make individuals mediocre but sociable and useful to the community, such as kindness, modesty, industriousness, generosity and pity, are glorified by the herd as human virtues (*BGE* 199).

Having tamed by guilt those whose instinct is to command, the democratic movement indulges in two interrelated types of morality: "the morality of timidity" and the "religion of pity" (*BGE* 201, 202). The aim of the morality of timidity, according to Nietzsche, is freedom from fear through the abolition of all danger and harshness from the world. The extreme manifestation in the modern world of this desire to be free from fear is pity for criminals and opposition to all harsh punishments. According to Nietzsche, "punishing somehow seems unfair [and] arouses fear" in "pathologically soft" societies which simply wish to render criminals "undangerous" (*BGE* 201). Society, therefore, according to the democrat, should not seek to punish criminals but simply reform them. Nietzsche's argument with regard to the democratic movement's attitude toward punishment is twofold. First, Nietzsche implies that when the community punishes crime they affirm their own moral code or beliefs about right and wrong. Nietzsche thinks this is good and healthy, but democrats do not like strong moral codes, believing that unless one's moral code is that no one should believe too strongly in one's moral code, you are a dangerous fanatic. Second, for Nietzsche and for democrats, punishment is commander-like. When the community punishes it affirms their feeling of superiority over the punished, harshness or hardness of feeling toward the punished flowing from the inequality of aristocratic societies. Democrats who oppose the punishment of criminals, on the other hand, tend to see themselves in the punished, such feeling of equality allowing for pity to flow for criminals.

The "religion of pity" is the second aspect of democratic morality. The aim of the religion of pity is freedom from all pain and suffering caused, for instance, by war, hunger, disease, poverty, and political and social oppression. Nietzsche thus argues that the democratic movement is united "in the cry and the impatience of pity, in their deadly hatred of suffering generally, in their almost feminine inability to remain spectators, to *let* someone suffer" (*BGE* 202). The problem with the attempt to end pain and suffering, as with the attempt to end danger and fear, Nietzsche implies, is that it is actually an attempt to drive all of the higher human types from the world along with their instinct of command. It is the commanders with their dangerous drives who are the cause of pain and suffering, lacking pity or compassion for those they harm due to their feeling of distance from them. For Nietzsche, however, a world without these higher types would be without any true human virtue or greatness. Either they are the ones who display such excellence or create conditions for excellence, such as courage, fortitude, endurance, to be manifested in others.

Dismayed that the democratic movement may cause the permanent diminution of the human species, at the end of Part Five Nietzsche directs our gaze toward philosophers of the future who will accomplish a new inversion of values and the "free spirits" who will precede them (*BGE* 203). Who are the philosophers of the future and what is their task? Will overturning democratic morality mean overturning democracy itself? Also, who are the free spirits and what conditions must they create to allow for the philosopher of the future to appear. Nietzsche turns to these questions in Part Nine of *Beyond Good and Evil*.

THE NOBLE AS ALTERNATIVE TO THE GOOD
AND THE END OF EVIL

In Part Nine of *Beyond Good and Evil*, "What is Noble," Nietzsche's alternative to democratic morality begins to appear. Closely linked to his concept of aristocracy, Nietzsche argues that by widening and maintaining the distance between different classes of human beings, aristocracy enhances the "type man" because it widens the distances within the soul itself (*BGE* 257). Whereas democracy flattens the soul because, insisting on equality, it flattens the ranks, aristocracy, separating men from men, separates the parts or deepens the soul itself. The depth and health of the soul, arising from the inequality between human beings, for Nietzsche means that the essence of life is struggle or, as we saw at the beginning of Part Five, the will to power. Thus, Nietzsche states that every healthy aristocracy, "will have to be an incarnate will to power [. . .] striv[ing] to grow, spread, seize, become predominant— not from any morality or immorality but because it is living and because life simply is will to power" (*BGE* 259). Inequality and exploitation, therefore, "belongs to the essence of what lives, as a basic organic function," and as such is amoral, or beyond questions of good and evil (*BGE* 259).

A problem has thus appeared at the beginning of Part Nine. In Part Five, Nietzsche stresses that human striving and excellence requires the sublimating pressure of narrow moral horizons and strict moral codes. Yet, at the beginning of Part Nine, Nietzsche claims that the brute fact of life is that its essence is an amoral will to power; health and depth in the soul arises out of the "survival of the fittest," as it were, and the attempt to end amoral exploitation is an attempt to deny life. The problem is therefore this: How do you derive the grounds for a morality after you recognize the brute fact that the essence of life is an amoral will to power and exploitation?[8] Nietzsche believes he provides a solution to this problem in what he labels "master morality" (*BGE* 260).

Nietzsche claims that through his consideration of various moral codes across space and time, he has discovered "two basic types" that run throughout: "master morality and slave morality" (BGE 204). Moral "values," therefore, originate, "either among a ruling group whose consciousness of its difference from the ruled group was accompanied by delight—or among the ruled, the slaves and dependents of every degree" (*BGE* 260). Moreover, such values, Nietzsche argues, always initially apply to persons, and only later to the actions practiced by such persons (*BGE* 260). Of persons, master morality designates them not as "good" and "bad," but rather in place of good and bad conceives of human being as "noble" and "contemptible" (*BGE* 260). In master morality the noble replaces the good, and it is the noble human being who is held up for praise and emulation.

The noble human being, according to Nietzsche, "experiences itself as determining values," and judges, "what is harmful to me is harmful in itself" (*BGE* 260). The noble person is therefore "value-creating," judging and designating others as noble or contemptible, and not judged or designated by them (*BGE* 260).[9] The noble judges everyone in relation to himself, and those who are like him are honored, those who are not are despised. Master morality is therefore a morality of "self-glorification," in which the noble human being experiences himself as the ultimate standard and center of the universe (*BGE* 260). The noble human being, Nietzsche argues, regards himself and those he honors as courageous, truthful, and "powerful," or hard both with himself and over others, praying, as an old Scandinavian saga has it, "A hard heart Wotan put into my breast" (*BGE* 260). Hard-hearted the noble lacks pity and compassion, inspires fear, and is proud and supremely self-confident. Perhaps most interestingly, Nietzsche claims, "it is the powerful who understand how to honor; this is their art, their realm of invention" (*BGE* 260). Inventing honor, the noble directs this art to a reverence for tradition that exposes a "prejudice in favor of the ancestors," resisting as contemptible "progress" and change (*BGE* 260). For Nietzsche, it seems that the past is more of our own or belongs to us more than the future which, potentially wide open and as yet not traversed, is not us. Thus, in honoring the past we honor ourselves, suiting the morality of "self-glorification" of the nobles.

Nietzsche elaborates on the noble's art of honoring when he claims that, "a sign of high rank" is "an instinct for rank" that "delight[s] in the nuances of reverence" (*BGE* 263). Arguing that the "height of a soul is tested dangerously when something of the first rank passes by," Nietzsche claims that, "reverence for the Bible [. . .] in Europe," taught by Christianity, beneficially cultivated in the masses "the feeling [. . .] that they are not to touch everything; that there are holy experiences before which they have to take off their shoes and keep away their unclean hands—this is almost their greatest advance toward humanity" (*BGE* 263). The "common people," therefore, according to Nietzsche, to the extent that they are still under the influence of scriptural religion, possess "more relative nobility of taste" than "so-called educated people and believers in 'modern ideas,'" whose "lack of modesty and comfortable insolence of their eyes and hands with which they touch, lick, and finger everything," Nietzsche finds "nauseous" (*BGE* 263).

The reverence for persons and things of high rank is illustrative of the noble's sense of separation between high and low. A shadow or imitation of this is shown by the many when they revere scripture, impressing on them the distinction between the "holy" and the profane, the clean and the unclean. The noble, therefore, has an instinct for separation; a separateness that keeps them and their peers distinct from their servants and slaves, giving an appreciation for rank that will prevent mixing with the contemptible. The contemptible person is everything the noble is not. From the perspective of the noble human being the contemptible are cowardly and, humbling themselves, are "doglike people who allow themselves to be maltreated" (*BGE* 260). They are liars, as it is "part of the fundamental faith of all aristocrats that the common people lie" (*BGE* 260). The contemptible are weak and soft-hearted, thereby inclined to pity and compassion, and, having no love for who and what they are and where they come from, are the "men of modern ideas," "progress," and "the future" (*BGE* 260). Thus, they have no idea of what it is to honor, and have no instinct for rank or reverence, belying the ignobility and self-loathing within their souls.

Nietzsche acknowledges that the morality of the nobles, their values and tastes, is alien to the tastes of the modern democratic movement. Asserting the distinction between the familiar and the foreign, the high and low, and thus rejecting the equality and cosmopolitanism of democracy, master morality insists, "one has duties only to one's peers; that against beings of a lower rank, against everything alien, one behave as one pleases or 'as the heart desires,' and in any case 'beyond good and evil'." (*BGE* 260).

The origin of "that famous opposition" between "good" and "evil," Nietzsche claims, is in slave morality, the morality of the ruled and oppressed (*BGE* 260). Nietzsche, by using the term "evil" in his discussion of the two categories within slave morality rather than the "bad," the latter substituted for the "contemptible" within master morality, draws attention to the fact that the noble has no idea of "evil;" "evil" is an invention of the oppressed. Having no concept of evil, the noble, Nietzsche implies, has no concept of, or at least no real respect for, a superior God. Thus, Nietzsche argues, "The noble soul gives as it takes, from that passionate and irritable instinct of repayment that lies in its depth. The concept of 'grace' has no meaning or good odor [among equals]" (*BGE* 265). As grace is a gift from God that cannot be repaid, the noble, wanting to be equal to God, as it were, either denies or resists it. Since the noble, "does not like to look 'up' [. . .] know[ing] itself to be at a height," they think of themselves, and not God, as the highest creator of values.

The meaning of "evil," therefore, also differs significantly from the "bad." The difference, Nietzsche implies, lies in the fact that unlike that which is merely "bad," that which is "evil" has a religious connotation. Applied originally to persons, the "evil" are in violation, it seems, of a divine command or of God's law; when they act they "sin" and not simply exploit or oppress. Thus, what are the oppressed doing when they invent the term "evil"? They are asserting, Nietzsche suggests, that there is a just God who cares about them governing the universe. The essence of life, therefore, is not the brutal will to power of the noble masters; the masters will be punished by an all-powerful and superior God for their exploitation of the powerless and oppressed. Nietzsche's implication is that the oppressed hide their value-creation or their desire, like the masters, to oppress others, in an omnipotent God that they also create and who they claim gave them their laws.[10] In this fundamental sense the oppressed are "liars," as the noble always suspects.

Slave morality designates those persons as "good" who make the ruled feel safe and secure. The good, therefore, are weak and undangerous, showing "pity, the complaisant and obliging hand, the warm heart, patience, industry, humility, and friendliness" (*BGE* 260). Also, since strength of intelligence can manifest a fearful inequality, Nietzsche argues that, "wherever slave morality becomes preponderant, language tends to bring the words 'good' and 'stupid' closer together" (BGE 207). Finally, the good possess a longing for freedom (*BGE* 260). Suffering for so long under the pressure of exploitation, the oppressed long to dispense with all rules and commitments that constrain one to obey, and to dispense with the past that one cannot change and thus adherence to which, they believe, limits one's freedom of action.

Persons who are "evil," according to slave morality, inspire fear and a sense of danger in the weak. Evil persons are thus able to project a sense of their own power and, "a certain terribleness, subtlety, and strength that does not permit contempt to develop" (*BGE* 260). The evil are also intelligent, and, sensing that they only obey laws that they give to themselves unlike the oppressed who always obey laws given by others, the evil, to feel their own power over themselves, have a longing for devotion; a longing to commit themselves to a person or a cause. Thus, Nietzsche claims, "love as passion—which is our European specialty—simply must be of noble origin" (*BGE* 260). In their most benign form, therefore, the evil are knights in shining armor, as it were, who devote themselves to damsels in distress. In their least benign form, perhaps, they appear to the weak as zealots or "fundamentalists" dedicated to narrow or exclusive religious or political causes.

The aim of the morality of the weak is utility, or to "ease the existence of those who suffer" (*BGE* 260). The weak also aim to convince themselves with their morality that it is better to be one of the humble and oppressed; that the nobles are not really happy but rather suffering in their own private "hell," as it were.

SOCRATES, DIONYSUS AND THE NOBLE IN MODERN TIMES

Can the noble be brought into our world today? If it can be reborn and is not gone forever, how so? Does the rebirth of the noble require a new politics, such that Nietzsche is calling for an end to democracy and a return to aristocracy with its class hierarchies, inequality and exploitation? Or, does the noble require a new art form akin to the tragedy of ancient Greece? In aphorism 295, the second last of the work, Nietzsche appears to invoke the Greek god Dionysus, the god, as we learn in *The Birth of Tragedy*, that Greek tragedy brought to the surface (*BGE* 295). At the end of *Beyond Good and Evil*, therefore, Nietzsche returns to Dionysus. Acknowledging that, "you [free spirits] no longer like to believe in God or gods," Nietzsche thus appears to call for a new art form that, like ancient tragedy, appeals to and heightens the sexual longings of the body (*BGE* 295, *BT* 24). These are the questions that Nietzsche turns to in the latter half of Part Nine.

Nietzsche addresses the question of democracy and whether it should be overturned in aphorism 269, when he analyzes the "psychologist" or "unriddler of souls" (*BGE* 269). Such a reader of souls, according to Nietzsche, sees that "the corruption, the ruination of the higher men, of the souls of a stranger type, is the rule" (*BGE* 269). Thus, whereas "the crowd, the educated, the enthusiasts" venerate the "great men" as gods, the psychologist "might suffocate from pity," and has learned to feel toward the great men "the greatest pity coupled with the greatest contempt" (*BGE* 269). The psychologist, therefore, is characterized by a mixture of slave qualities, in the capacity for pity, and master qualities, in the feeling of contempt. In this way the psychologist is surprisingly like the great whom they observe, the latter apparently harboring a secret slave quality hitherto concealed in the discussion. According to Nietzsche, "the 'god' was merely a poor sacrificial animal. Success has always been the greatest liar—and the 'work' itself is a success; the great statesman, the conqueror, the discoverer is disguised by his creations, often beyond recognition; the 'work' [. . .] of the artist or the philosopher, invents the man who created it [. . .] 'great men' [. . .] are subsequent pieces of minor fiction" (*BGE* 269). Thus, having begun with the persons of the great when discussing master morality, Nietzsche now moves to the actions of the great in a way that diminishes the persons. The actions of noble human beings are now seen as "works" meant to improve upon and hence conceal the inner being of the performer. The noble human being therefore, in their works, creates masks or disguises to conceal their true character; like the common people they contemn they are, so to speak, "liars."

The suffocating pity that the psychologist has for the great, moreover, makes them like women, who in Nietzsche's eyes tend to give great men "eruptions of boundless and most devoted pity" (*BGE* 269). Yet, woman's pity, which is the way she loves, according to Nietzsche, "deceives itself regularly about its power; woman would like to believe that love can achieve anything—that is her characteristic faith" (*BGE* 269). The "higher" types evoke such pity and love from psychologists and women, Nietzsche suggests, because they inevitably seek death. Nietzsche gives Jesus as the exemplar of the higher type in this regard, and his "holy fable and disguise"—that he was the son of God sacrificed on the cross to redeem the sins of mankind—as the greatest of masks (*BGE* 269). As "one of the most painful cases of the martyrdom of knowledge about love," Jesus, Nietzsche claims, demanded absolute love from human beings but discovers as a result, the defectiveness of human love. Perhaps human beings can never love another more than they love themselves (*BGE* 269). The imperfection of human love leads Jesus to invent a God who, as perfect love, demands the former's sacrifice on the cross to redeem these imperfect human beings (*BGE* 269). Thus, whereas

Kierkegaard in *Philosophical Fragments* emphasizes the birth of Jesus as flowing from the fact that God is love, Nietzsche emphasizes Jesus's death.

Through his discussion of Jesus as an exemplar of the higher types pitied by psychologists and women, Nietzsche suggests that even the "masters" have been impacted and transformed by "slave" morality. Like Jesus, they now demand love or boundless pity, a slave characteristic. Imitating another slave characteristic, they create God(s) to punish those who hurt them, and they are liars who invent masks and disguises to conceal their inner being. Moreover, such conflicted higher types, as it were, seek self-destruction, suggesting natural masters are more likely to disappear than endure to impose a new order on the world. Nietzsche, therefore, shows us that the noble is not going to be revived in the modern age by retuning to an older aristocratic order, but rather the noble will have to arise out of democracy itself.

It is when hoping for the re-emergence of the noble out of the democratic order that the transition to actions and away from characteristics of persons is most useful. If the noble is understood not as a person but an action, it may be possible for common persons in the democracy to manifest nobility. What types of activities or ways of living in a democratic age manifest nobility? Anything which separates or distinguishes one human being from another, isolating them or raising them above the crowd, as it were. Thus, Nietzsche argues that the claim to extreme suffering is a claim to nobility in a democratic age. The sufferer, or the "survivor" as we would say today, having the "spiritual [. . .] haughtiness" and pride that comes from being one of "the elect of knowledge," believes, "that by virtue of his suffering he knows more than the cleverest and wisest could possibly know, [. . .] he [. . .] has once been 'at home' in many distant, terrifying worlds of which 'you know nothing'" (*BGE* 270). According to Nietzsche, "profound suffering makes noble; it separates" (*BGE* 270). In what appears to be an opposite claim to distinction, the "cheerfulness" of the "scientific men" or the insolence of the cynic, both of whom possess "a certain ostentatious courage of taste which takes suffering casually," use their cheerfulness or insolence as masks to hide the true suffering of their souls, thereby nobly separating themselves from others (*BGE* 270).

The "instinct of cleanliness," the instinct of the "saints," and the hatred of other people's "smell" as a manifestation of our bodily nature, according to Nietzsche, "places those possessed of it in the oddest and most dangerous lonesomeness" (*BGE* 271). Thus for Nietzsche, the overbearing concern for hygiene and good grooming, as it were, is a, "propensity [that] distinguishes—it is a noble propensity—it also separates" (*BGE* 271). Other "signs of nobility" in a democratic age, according to Nietzsche, is a form of nationalism that is anti-cosmopolitan, hence "never thinking of degrading our duties into duties for everybody [. . .] counting one's privileges and their exercise among one's duties," thereby maintaining the distinction between one's own people and others (*BGE* 271). Another sign of nobility is ambition or the striving for something great, as someone who strives for the top, an activity of the lowly rather than the high, "considers everyone he meets along the way either as a means or as a delay and obstacle—[. . .] spoil[ing] all of his relations to others" (*BGE* 273). Such a person, therefore, "knows solitude and what is most poisonous in it" (BGE 274).

Nietzsche suggests that those in a democratic age who seek distinction from the crowd, as it were, encourage the notion of separation and hence inequality between human beings. In this sense, they are like the free spirits Nietzsche addresses in Part Five, who create the conditions for the coming of the philosopher of the future who will bring an alternative to democratic morality, thereby halting if not reversing the degeneration of the human species. Perhaps most interestingly in this regard, Nietzsche suggests that separation and thus nobility in the modern era can be achieved through philosophy. Identifying the philosopher with the "hermit," Nietzsche says:

> The hermit does not believe that any philosopher—assuming that every philosopher was first of all a hermit—ever expressed his real and ultimate opinions in books: does one not write books precisely to conceal what one harbors? [. . .] Every philosophy is a foreground philosophy[. . . .] Every philosophy also conceals a philosophy; every opinion is also a hideout, every word also a mask (*BGE* 289).

The activity of philosophy for Nietzsche, which he couples with writing books, perhaps books like his own, is by nature ironic; it always conceals as well as reveals the mind of the philosopher, thereby maintaining the separation between the philosopher and their fellows as it simultaneously unites them in rational dialogue. Such an ironic way of writing books that reveals and conceals the philosopher at the same time, reminds us of Plato who, concealing himself in the interlocutors whom he writes into his dialogues, never actually appears himself. We are reminded of Kierkegaard's argument in the *Concept of Irony* that in his dialogues, Plato tried to become one with his teacher, Socrates. Moreover, according to Kierkegaard, Socrates like Plato is also ironic, living an "existential" irony whereby he reveals and conceals himself from others simultaneously, thereby asserting his subjectivity against the moral and political order of his time. Is Nietzsche, like Kierkegaard, in the end pointing us to Socrates and Socratic philosophy as that which will cause the noble to once again arise in a democratic age?[11] Is a new "Socrates" the philosopher of the future whose way has been prepared by the free spirits? Although Nietzsche critiques the Socrates of Athens for being dishonest and destructive of noble Athenians' belief in their aristocratic moral code, perhaps a new Socrates, or the return of Socratic dialectic in our time, can be helpful in leading democrats to question the dominant moral code of the democratic age, therefore opening us to the noble.

The possibility that Socrates is the philosopher of the future through which nobility will be reborn, brings us to the invocation of Dionysus with which *Beyond Good and Evil* concludes. In aphorism 295, Nietzsche addresses Dionysus as both a "deity and philosopher" and as "lacking in shame," and reports that the god told him, "I often reflect how I might yet advance [the animal man] and make him stronger, more evil, and more profound than he is" (BGE 236). To this Nietzsche asks, startled: "Stronger, more evil, and more profound?" Dionysus: "Yes, [. . .] stronger, more evil, and more profound, also more beautiful" (*BGE* 295). Dionysus, therefore, lacking shame, like Aeschylus who put original sin in the male Prometheus rather than the female Eve, will delight in or celebrate human "evil" rather than condemn it as slave morality had done. Moreover, since everything noble human beings are is "evil," this new celebration of evil can lead human beings to aspire to be more beautiful and more profound.

Nietzsche, however, also addresses Dionysus as a philosopher and not simply a deity. Thus, it appears that Nietzsche may be calling for more than the revival of a Dionysian art form that gets us in touch with the sexual longings of our bodies, but also for the return of an ancient philosophy or classical rationalism in our democratic age. As a philosopher, Nietzsche says of Dionysus that he is:

> The genius of the heart from whose touch everyone walks away richer, not having received grace and surprised, not as blessed and oppressed by alien goods, but richer in himself, newer to himself than before, broken open, blown at and sounded out by a thawing wind, perhaps more unsure, tenderer, more fragile, more broken, but full of hopes that as yet have no name, full of new will and currents, full of new dissatisfaction and undertows—but what am I doing my friends? (BGE 295).

Dionysus the philosopher, breaking open and blowing out all those he touches, empties his interlocutors of the opinions that they had within. Therefore, like the god in Kierkegaard's *Philosophical Fragments*, Dionysus reveals to you that you do not have the truth, that you are untruth, or that you do not know what you thought you knew. Dionysus, in other words, is like the Socrates of the *Apology* and many other Platonic dialogues, who gives his interlocutors knowledge of ignorance.[12] Such a Dionysian Socrates, Nietzsche suggests, through questioning can cause his interlocutors to lose faith in the old truths, as it were, or the truths of the contemporary democratic morality. Yet, "full of hopes that as yet have no name, full of new will and currents," the interlocutor, having been shown their ignorance and thus no longer believing that democratic values are the only human values simply, is prepared to turn to the new or, in "noble" fashion, "return" to the old in a future world. Nietzsche, therefore, points us to the Platonic dialogues to be touched by the Socrates we find there. Engaging in dialogue with Socrates, we will be liberated from the cave of good and evil and the chains of the democratic movement, freed to strive upward for the noble.

NOTES

1. For an alternative interpretation see Villa, who argues that for Nietzsche Socrates is the exemplar of intellectual honesty, not dishonesty. Villa, *Socratic Citizenship*, 128.

2. See Lampert, *Nietzsche's Task*, 156–58. Zuckert argues that Nietzsche attributes both belief in the necessity of lying and the search for the idea of the Good to Plato, not Socrates. Zuckert, *Postmodern Platos*, 17–18, 21–22.

3. Jeffrey Church, *Nietzsche's Culture of Humanity: Beyond Aristocracy and Democracy in the Early Period*. (New York: Cambridge University Press, 2015), 4–5.

4. Ibid., 2. For a similar argument with respect to culture, see Bertram, *Nietzsche*, 274–76; and Villa, *Socratic Citizenship*, 148–55.

5. Church, *Nietzsche's Culture of Humanity*, 97–100.

6. See Laurence Lampert, *Nietzsche's Task: An Interpretation of* Beyond Good and Evil (New Haven: Yale University Press, 2001), 151–52. For an alternative reading, see Church, *Nietzsche's Culture of Humanity*, 4.

7. But see Church, who helpfully suggests that the narrowing of horizons to which Nietzsche refers in the passage in question is not with reference to the political community but to a new community of culture. Church, *Nietzsche's Culture of Humanity*, 2.

8. Also see Lampert, *Nietzsche's Task*, 152.

9. Zuckert references Nietzsche's understanding of the noble as value-creating when she argues that for Nietzsche the proper work of the philosopher is "legislation." Zuckert, *Postmodern Platos*, 22.

10. Villa gives an alternative interpretation, arguing that Nietzsche opposes "slave morality" not for is content, but rather its form; it presents its moral code as the one true moral code, thus denying the legitimacy of moral pluralism and tolerance. Villa, *Socratic Citizenship*, 147.

11. See Church, who argues that Socrates is one of Nietzsche's "exemplary individuals," manifesting both the meritocratic and democratic aspects of culture. Church, *Nietzsche's Culture of Humanity*, 7, 97–100. For an alternative view, see Lampert who argues that "Platonism" is still the opponent in the last five chapters of Nietzsche's work. Lampert, *Nietzsche's Task*, 147.

12. Also see Bertram, who argues that this image of Dionysus evokes not only a Socratic philosopher, but the philosopher Nietzsche himself. Bertram, *Nietzsche*, 254.

Conclusion

The Socratic Soul in a Democratic Age

This study began by noting that students of Leo Strauss can be distinguished by their commitment to classical rationalism, following Strauss himself in their attempt to revive the classical political philosophy of Plato's Socrates. Strauss's turn to Socrates, however, is itself a manifestation of a philosophic movement that began in the nineteenth century to recover and revive the practice of Socratic philosophy in our democratic age. Reacting against Hegel's deification of the modern state, philosophers such as Kierkegaard, Mill and Nietzsche turn to Socrates and the Socratic philosopher as exemplars of the beauty of individuality that can be held up against the totalizing attempts of the state and the concomitant belief that history has come to an "end."

Strauss's recovery of Socratic philosophy, however, is innovative in a crucial respect. Through his readings of the Platonic dialogues Strauss came to question whether Socrates actually meant his teaching on the ideas to be taken seriously by the careful listener. Indeed, in *The City and Man*, Strauss goes so far as to assert that Socrates' theory of ideas, "is very hard to understand; to begin with, it is utterly incredible, not to say that it appears to be fantastic," and that, "no one has succeeded in giving a satisfactory or clear account of this doctrine of ideas."[1] Scholars such as Catherine Zuckert argue that for Strauss the Socratic "doctrines" of the rational soul and the ideas were mere "public teachings" on the part of Socrates designed to support the belief in justice and therewith the necessary conditions for philosophic inquiry.[2] Zuckert concludes, therefore, that for Strauss Socratic philosophy was not constituted by a set of doctrines but rather was primarily a way of life embodied by the person of Socrates.[3] Similarly, Thomas Pangle argues that Strauss rejected the "theological dimension" of the ideas as entities which are "self-subsisting, being at home as it were in an entirely different place from human beings."[4] For Strauss, according to Pangle, the self-subsisting nature of the ideas are salutary Socratic myths for the education of young people.[5]

In calling into question how seriously Socrates meant his teachings on the rational human soul and the ides to be taken, Strauss indicates that Hegel misunderstood Socratic philosophy. As we have seen, Hegel argues that Socrates advanced beyond Anaxagoras by connecting universal reason to concrete human particulars, through his theory of ideas. In doing so Socrates reorients philosophy away from the study of material nature to the nature of the soul as it is drawn toward the good. Yet, the modern liberal state as the "divine idea as it exists on earth," emerging at the end of history, must be protected from the corrosive effects of Socratic philosophizing about the ideas. The ideas are destructive to political society, according to Hegel, because they replace the actions of virtue for speech about it and create a split between the reality of a people's virtues and the idealized versions of them which can never be lived up to. Socratic philosophy, therefore, must come to an end with the perfection of history. Strauss, however, suggests that Hegel mistook the public teaching—the rational soul and the ideas—for the core of Socratic philosophy.[6] The core of Socratic philosophy is a way of life embodied by Socrates and not the rational comprehension of universal truths as the latter are understood by Hegel.

In suggesting that the rational soul grasping the universal ideas is a "public teaching" meant to be seen through by the serious student of Socrates, Strauss, if not entirely subordinating it to passion, displaces the authority of reason in the Socratic philosopher's soul. The type of reason that only grasps things in the form of universality separate from matter as Hegel would have it, is certainly called into question. Strauss, therefore, suggests a conception of the philosophic soul that is similar to that held by Kierkegaard, Mill and Nietzsche.

In *Fear and Trembling*, Kierkegaard argues that Abraham transcends the rational moral order embodied by his community, thereby isolating himself as a single individual above the universal who enters into a personal relationship with God. In doing so, Abraham acquires a higher individuality based in the passions of the soul as opposed to the lower passions of the body. Abraham learns that the soul is erotic as well as rational, is heart as well as mind, and thus unites the two parts of the soul, passion and reason or love and thought, with passion and love understood as the higher part of the soul. Similarly, as an intellectual tragic hero Socrates, according to Kierkegaard, doubts the universal and grasps at a particular subjectivity which is beyond it, therefore understanding the core of the soul as passion rather than reason. Moreover, as an intellectual tragic hero Socrates, speaking ironically after he receives his death sentence, has last words whereby he affirms himself as an individual above the universal. Irony is a form of speech that allows Socrates to communicate his passionate subjectivity to others. Yet, Kierkegaard argues that Abraham, the father of faith, also has last words before the intended sacrifice of Isaac: "God himself will provide the lamb for the burnt offering, my son." Like Socrates' speech Abraham's speech is ironic, and thus it turns out that *Fear and Trembling*, which begins as a eulogy to Abraham, can also be understood as a eulogy to Socrates.

John Stuart Mill, in *On Liberty*, like Kierkegaard locates greatness, as it were, not in a universal reason that makes human beings the same, but rather in the passions that make them different and set some unique but indispensable individuals apart from the social and moral norms of their time. According to Mill, the main danger in our democratic age is that individual exceptionalism and idiosyncrasy will be crushed by the weight of a social tyranny more formidable than many kinds of political oppression. In order to prevent the enforced conformity to society's ideas and practices, the freedom of each individual to say and do as they think fit, provided they do not harm others in the process, must be protected. Liberal freedom allows each to construct their own unique, individual identity without fear of social stigma. Moreover, the individuality that liberal freedom makes possible, according to Mill, arises from erotic desires and impulses understood to form the core of the soul which, properly sublimated, are the cause of intellectual energy an exceptional individual may have.

In *The Birth of Tragedy*, Nietzsche, like Kierkegaard and Mill, seeks to displace the authority of reason in order to get exceptional human beings back in touch with not simply their passions, but, going further, their bodies and its sexual longing for unity with the material whole. To do so, according to Nietzsche, Socratic rationalism, which seeks to master the body, must be rejected so that there can return to the Dionysian celebration of the sexual power of nature. Yet, when Nietzsche concludes *Beyond Good and Evil*, he invokes Dionysus in such a way that this god is presented as practicing a Socratic dialectic that makes us aware of our ignorance. Thus, just as we discover that Kierkegaard's eulogy to Abraham is also meant as a eulogy to Socrates, it comes to light that Nietzsche's invocation of Dionysus is actually a call to revive a Socratic form of philosophy. Moreover, Nietzsche's assessment in *Beyond Good and Evil* of the conclusions of Socratic dialectic, sounds very similar to Strauss's argument that Socrates intended his serious students to understand that his many discussions of the rational soul grasping the ideas is mere "public teaching" that does not get to the core of his philosophy. According to Nietzsche, Socrates spent his life laughing at noble Athenians who, in response to his question "Why?," could not give sufficient reasons for their actions. Yet, Nietzsche argues that upon self-examination Socrates discovered the same difficulty in giving a rational account for his actions. Socrates, in other words, discovers the non-rational, instinctive grounding for all apparently "rational" moral judgments. For Nietzsche, therefore, Socrates, had "at bottom, [. . .] seen through the irrational element in moral judgments" (*BGE* 191).

Strauss, as the discussion above emphasizes, seeks to put a distance in his readers' minds between Socrates and his apparent theory of ideas. In doing so, Strauss, I believe, of the philosophers explored in this study comes closest to Kierkegaard. For instance, in the *Concept of Irony*, Kierkegaard argues that Socrates practices an "ironic" method of questioning that posits questions not designed to bring forth answers, but rather to show that there are no answers, as it were; there is no truth or objective reality that the human mind can grasp. Plato, on the other hand, practices a "speculative" method of questioning that posits questions that can and should be answered, and when the answer is given we have acquired knowledge of the subject at hand. In other words, when Socrates asks, "What is . . .?," Plato, unintended by his teacher, answers "It is . . ." How does Plato answer Socrates' questions, according to Kierkegaard? With the ideas or forms. The theory of ideas, therefore, belongs to Plato and not Socrates.

Kierkegaard provides evidence for his view that ideas are Platonic rather than Socratic in his interpretation of Alcibiades' erotic attachment to Socrates so forcefully on display in Plato's *Symposium*. According to Kierkegaard, in this dialogue Socrates is presented as the embodiment of *eros* and therefore longing for something outside of himself, but empty of ideas has no object toward which to direct his longings. However, for precisely this reason he is also the object of *eros*. If Socrates could have helped Alcibiades ascend to the idea of the beautiful, Alcibiades would have loved the idea and not exclusively the person of Socrates himself. Without the idea, Alcibiades is left with only the particular individual to love, which is painful and hard.

Although both Strauss and Kierkegaard believe that the ideas are not truly Socratic, there are important differences between the two thinkers. First, whereas Kierkegaard seeks to disentangle Socrates from Plato by denying that the ideas are Socratic, Strauss's intention is to disentangle Socrates not from Plato, both of whom he treats as one, but rather from Christianity.[7] For example, medieval thinkers such as St. Augustine for centuries equated Socrates' concept of the idea of good with the God whom they believed brought into being and grounded both the natural and moral orders.[8] Thus, in undermining the intellectual status of the ideas it is apparent that Strauss wishes to revive a Socratic philosophy in our time that is free from association with Christian doctrine. This leads to the second important difference between Strauss and Kierkegaard. For Kierkegaard, unlike the "Platonic" Socrates, as it were, who teaches the theory of ideas, a truly "Socratic" Socrates without ideas is much closer to Christianity than Strauss believes.

The close relationship between the "Socratic" Socrates and Christianity is brought to light by Kierkegaard in *Philosophical Fragments*. In this work, Kierkegaard explores the relation between philosophy and faith by contrasting Socrates and the "god" as teachers. When Socrates is the teacher of a philosophic learner, according to Kierkegaard, Socrates' method of questioning is the occasion for both student and teacher to recollect truths that were already in their souls but which they had forgotten were there. When questioned in the right way, the truths that the philosophic learner and teacher recollect are the universal ideas or forms. Thus, the Socrates of *Philosophical Fragments* resembles the Plato of *Concept of Irony*; he is, as it were, a "Platonic" Socrates with ideas. Moreover, in *Philosophical Fragments* Kierkegaard characterizes the self-knowledge or knowledge of our souls that comes when we recollect the ideas within them, as "God knowledge" (*PF* 11). Kierkegaard's suggestion is that for philosophic learners who recollect the ideas, the highest form of human knowledge is knowledge of the self—of the truth within the self and that the truth is within the self—and not knowledge of the other or the higher than the self. Thus, Kierkegaard suggests in contrast to Strauss that a philosophy centered around the theory of ideas will pull its adherents away from, not closer to, Christianity, or away from any way of life that embraces the existence of a god distinct from or higher than the human. "Platonic" ideas, as it were, direct philosophic *eros* to the ideas, accessible to human reason alone, and away from the god.

When, on the other hand, the god is teacher of a religious learner according to Kierkegaard, the god does not cause the learner to recollect a universal idea that is within the self, but rather brings knowledge of a truth that is beyond the self; of a passionate particularity or subjectivity that exists beyond the universal. Since the existence of such a passionate subjectivity beyond the universal is not accessible to human reason alone, its truth is a truth that only the god and god alone can give. Kierkegaard defines this passionate subjectivity beyond the universal as the "unknown" and gives the unknown the name "god" (*PF* 39). Ironically, therefore, when the god gives the truth he gives himself to the learner, and accepting the god, the learner receives the gift of faith. Moreover, not only is it the god who brings the truth to the learner but it is also the god, according to Kierkegaard, who is responsible for giving the leaner the condition for learning the truth. Since the condition for learning the truth is "being able to ask about it," it is apparent that the condition that the god gives is knowledge of ignorance; we learn that the truth is not within us but beyond us, that we are untruth or do not know what we think we know.

The "god" as teacher in *Philosophical Fragments* is very similar to the Socrates of the *Apology* to which Kierkegaard points. In showing his interlocutors that they do not know what they think they know, Socrates gives them knowledge of ignorance and thus, like the god, the condition for learning the truth. Moreover, Kierkegaard suggests the truth that Socrates is trying to bring to light for his interlocutors is the truth that the god brings to the person of faith. Socrates, according to Kierkegaard, in always keeping his own ignorance or knowledge of what he doesn't know in mind when he philosophizes, always keeps the unknown before him, as it were. The unknown, which Kierkegaard also names the "god," that Socrates keeps before him is something which reason cannot think but nonetheless has faith is there. Since reason, Kierkegaard argues, thinks in universal terms, it appears that the unknown it cannot think is a passionate particularity beyond the universal. Yet, Socrates, according to Kierkegaard, understands the awareness of an unknown, passionate subjectivity beyond the self as a metaphor for the awareness of an unknown, passionate subjectivity within the self. In revealing the truth to his interlocutors Socrates, in other words, reveals himself to them. It appears, therefore, that Socrates of the *Apology*, like the god, gives both the condition for learning the truth and the truth itself. Thus, just as we discover that the eulogy to Abraham in *Fear and Trembling* is in fact a eulogy to Socrates, so we discover that the god in *Philosophical Fragments* is also an image of Socrates. Moreover, the Socrates of whom the god is an image is the "Socratic" Socrates of the *Concept of Irony*, the Socrates without or separate from the universal ideas.

The connection between the "Socratic" Socrates of the *Concept of Irony* and the embodied god of *Philosophical Fragments* is further illustrated in the impact the embodied god has on the religious learner. For Kierkegaard, the truth that the embodied god teaches is not accessible to human reason, but can only be held by faith. Yet, since it is not accessible to reason, it cannot be separated from the divine teacher or thought independently by the learner. The embodied god does not give the learner a simple universal to think, but what appears to be a more absolute particularity beyond the universal which cannot be known in the strict sense but only felt. The learner, therefore, is "stuck," as it were, to the embodied god; they cannot move to a universal separate from or beyond the divine teacher. Faith, therefore, is not believing in what the embodied god says, for example the Sermon on the Mount, but simply that the embodied god is—the god become human. Thus, the learner of the embodied god is like the Alcibiades of the *Symposium* whom Kierkegaard discusses in the *Concept of Irony*. Alcibiades, according to Kierkegaard, cannot direct his love to a universal idea and hence remains "stuck," as it were, or erotically attached to the person of Socrates himself. Alcibiades' experience of love for the "Socratic" Socrates, therefore, is what Kierkegaard portrays in *Philosophical Fragments* as the experience of faith the learner has in the embodied god.

NOTES

1. Strauss, *The City and Man*, 119.
2. Zuckert, *Postmodern Platos*, 118, 154–55.
3. Zuckert, *Postmodern Platos*, 154–55.

4. Thomas L. Pangle, "Introduction," in Leo Strauss, *Studies in Platonic Political Philosophy* (Chicago: University of Chicago Press, 1983), 2–3.

5. Ibid., 3.

6. See Zuckert for a similar gloss on Heidegger and Derrida's critique of Socratic philosophy. Zuckert, *Postmodern Platos,* 155.

7. See Zuckert, *Postmodern Platos*, 110, 154–55.

8. Augustine, *The Confessions*, Maria Boulding trans. (New York: Vintage Spiritual Classics, 1997), 138–39.

Bibliography

Aeschylus. 1983. *Agamemnon,* trans. Hugh Lloyd Jones, Berkeley: University of California Press.

Agacinski, Sylvianne. *Aparte: Conceptions and Death of Soren Kierkegaard,* Kevin Newmark trans., Tallahassee: Florida State University Press.

Augustine. 1997. *The Confessions,* Maria Boulding trans. New York: Vintage Spiritual Classics.

Baldwin, Brigit. 1989. "Irony, that 'Little Invisible Personage': A Reading of Kierkegaard's Ghosts," *MLN* 104/5, Comparative Literature.

Bennett, Benjamin. 1979. "Nietzsche's Idea of Myth: The Birth of Tragedy from the Spirit of Eighteenth-Century Aesthetics," *PMLA* 94(3).

Bertram, Ernst. 2009. *Nietzsche: Attempt at a Mythology,* Robert E. Norton trans., Urbana: University of Illinois Press.

Church, Jeffrey. 2015. *Nietzsche's Culture of Humanity: Beyond Aristocracy and Democracy in the Early Period,* New York: Cambridge University Press, 2015.

———. 2011."Two concepts of culture in the early Nietzsche," *European Journal of Political Theory* 10/3.

Cross, Andrew. 1998. "Neither either nor or: The perils of reflexive irony," in *The Cambridge Companion to Kierkegaard,* Alastair Hannay and Gordon D. Mariono eds., Cambridge: Cambridge University Press.

Deinstag, Joshua Foa. 2004. "Tragedy, Pessimism, Nietzsche," *New Literary History,* 35/1.

De Tocqueville, Alexis. 1990. *Democracy in America,* Henry Reeve trans. (New York: Vintage Classics.

Dooley, Mark. 2001. *The Politics of Exodus: Soren Kierkegaard's Ethics of Responsibility,* New York: Fordham University Press.

Evans, C. Stephen. 1992. *Passionate Reason: Making Sense of Kierkegaard's Philosophical Fragments,* Bloomington: Indiana University Press, 1992.

Fenves, Peter. 1993. *"Chatter": Language and History in Kierkegaard,* Stanford: Stanford University Press.

Ferreira, M. Jamie. 1998. "Faith and the Kierkegaardian leap," in *The Cambridge Companion to Kierkegaard,* Alastair Hannay and Gordon D. Marion eds., Cambridge: Cambridge University Press.

Findlay. 1958. *Hegel: A Re-Examination,* London: George Allen & Unwin Ltd.

Gambino, Giacomo. 1996. "Nietzsche and the Greeks: Identity, Politics and Tragedy." *Polity* 28/4.

Green, Ronald M. 1998. "Developing Fear and Trembling," in *The Cambridge Companion to Kierkegaard*, Alastair Hannay and Gordon D. Marino eds., Cambridge: Cambridge University Press.

Hadot, Pierre. 2002. *What Is Ancient Philosophy?*, Michael Chase trans., Cambridge: Harvard University Press.

Hassner, Pierre. 1987. "Georg W.F. Hegel," Allan Bloom tans., in *History of Political Philosophy*, Leo Strauss and Joseph Cropsey eds., Chicago: University of Chicago Press.

Hegel, G.W.F. 1956. *The Philosophy of History*, J. Siberee trans., New York: Dover Publications.

Houlgate, Stephen. 2005. *An Introduction to Hegel: Freedom, Truth and History*, Malden, MA: Blackwell Publishing.

Howland, Jacob. 2006. *Kierkegaard and Socrates: A Study in Philosophy and Faith*, New York: Cambridge University Press.

Inwood, Michael. 1983. *Hegel*, Abingdon, Oxon: Routledge.

Jackson, Timothy P. 1998. "Arminian edification: Kierkegaard on grace and free will," in *The Cambridge Companion to Kierkegaard*, Alastair Hannay and Gordon D. Marion eds., Cambridge: Cambridge University Press.

Kierkegaard, Soren. 1989. the *Concept of Irony*, Howard V. Hong and Edna H. Hong trans. and eds., Princeton: Princeton University Press.

———. 1985. *Philosophical Fragments, or a Fragment of Philosophy*, Howard V. Hong and Edna H. Hong eds. and trans., Princeton: Princeton University Press.

———. 1983. *Fear and Trembling: Dialectical Lyric*, Howard V. Hong and Edna H. Hong trans., Princeton: Princeton University Press.

———. 1980.*The Sickness Unto Death*, Edward V. Hong and Edna H. Hong eds. and trans., Princeton: Princeton University Press.

Kofman. 1998. "Baubo: Theological Perversion and Fetishism," in *Feminist Interpretations of Friedrich Nietzsche*, Kelly Oliver and Marilyn Pearsall eds., University Park: Pennsylvania State University Press.

Lampert, Laurence. 2001. *Nietzsche's Task: An Interpretation of Beyond Good and Evil*, New Haven: Yale University Press.

———. 1996. *Leo Strauss and Nietzsche*, Chicago: University of Chicago Press.

———. 1993. *Nietzsche and Modern Times: a Study of Bacon, Descartes, and Nietzsche*, New Haven: Yale University Press.

Leon, Celine. 1998. "The No Woman's Land of Kierkegaardian Exceptions," in *Feminist Interpretations of Kierkegaard*, Celine Leon and Sylvia Walsh eds., University Park: Pennsylvania State University Press.

Makus, Ingrid. 2007. "Nietzsche's criticism of Socratic Reason and the Problem of Identity," in *Socrates: Reason or Unreason as the Foundation of European Identity*, Ann Ward ed., Newcastle, UK: Cambridge Scholars Publishing.

Marcuse, Herbert. 1960. *Reason and Revolution: Hegel and the Rise of Social Theory*, Boston: Beacon Press.

McCarney, Joseph. 2000. *Routledge Philosophy Guidebook to Hegel on History*, London: Routledge.

Mercer, David E. 2001. *Kierkegaard's Living Room: The Relation Between Faith and History in Philosophical Fragments*, Montreal and Kingston: McGill-Queen's University Press.

Mill, John Stuart. 1982. *On Liberty*, London: Penguin Books.

Mooney, Edward F. 1981. "Understanding Abraham: Care, Faith, and the Absurd," in *Kierkegaard's Fear and Trembling: Critical Appraisals,* Tuscaloosa, AL: University of Alabama Press.

Most, Glenn W. 2007. "Socrates in Hegel," in *Socrates in the Nineteenth and Twentieth Centuries*, M.B. Trapp ed., Aldershot, UK: Ashgate Publishing.

Nichols, Mary P. 1988. *Socrates and the Political Community: An Ancient Debate*, Albany: State University of New York Press.

———. 1997. "The Problem of Socrates," in *Twilight of the Idols*, Richard Polt trans., Indianapolis, IN: Hackett Publishing Company.

Nietzsche, Friedrich. 1967. *The Birth of Tragedy and the Case of Wagner.* Walter Kaufmann trans., New York: Vintage.

———. 1967. "Attempt at Self-Criticism," in *The Birth of Tragedy and the Case of Wagner.* Walter Kaufmann trans. New York: Vintage.

———. 1966. *Beyond Good and Evil: Prelude to a Philosophy of the Future,* Walter Kaufmann trans., New York: Vintage.

Oliver, Kelly and Pearsall, Marilyn. 1998. "Why Feminists Read Nietzsche," in *Feminist Interpretations of Friedrich Nietzsche,* Kelly Oliver and Marilyn Pearsall eds., University Park: Pennsylvania State University Press.

Owen. 1998, "Nietzsche's Squandered Seductions: Feminism, the Body, and the Politics of Genealogy," in *Feminist Interpretations of Friedrich Nietzsche,* Kelly Oliver and Marilyn Pearsall eds., University Park: Pennsylvania State University Press.

Pangle, Thomas L. 2006. *Leo Strauss: An Introduction to His Thought and Intellectual Legacy,* Baltimore: Johns Hopkins University Press.

———. 2003. *Political Philosophy and the God of Abraham,* Baltimore: The Johns Hopkins University Press.

———. 1983. "Introduction," in Leo Strauss, *Studies in Platonic Political Philosophy,* Chicago: University of Chicago Press.

Plato. 2002. *Apology.* G.M.A. Grube trans., Indianapolis: Hackett Publishing Company.

———. 2002. *Meno,* G.M.A. Grube trans., Indianapolis: Hackett Publishing Company.

———. 1998. *Phaedo,* Eva Brann, et. al. trans., Newburyport, MA: Focus Classical Library.

———. 1993. *Symposium,* Seth Benardete trans., Chicago: University of Chicago Press.

———. 1968. *Republic,* Allan Bloom trans., New York: Basic Books.

Riley, Jonathan. 2013. "Mill's Greek Ideal of Individuality," in *John Stuart Mill: A British Socrates,* Houndmills, UK: Palgrave Macmillan.

Ryan, Alan. 2013. "The Philosopher in the Agora," in *John Stuart Mill: A British Socrates,* Houndmills, UK: Palgrave Macmillan.

Sarf, Harold. 1983. "Reflections on Kierkegaard's Socrates," *Journal of the History of Ideas* 44/2.

Schutte, Ofelia. 1998. "Nietzsche's Politics," in *Feminist Interpretations of Friedrich Nietzsche,* Kelly Oliver and Marilyn Pearsall eds., University Park: Pennsylvania State University Press.

Smyth, John Vignaux. 1986. *A Question of Eros: Irony in Stern, Kierkegaard and Barthes,* Tallahassee: Florida State University Press.

Speight, Allen. 2008. *The Philosophy of Hegel,* Montreal & Kingston: McGill-Queen's University Press.

Stern, Paul. 1993. *Socratic Rationalism and Political Philosophy: An Interpretation of Plato's Phaedo,* Albany: State University of New York Press.

Strauss, Leo. 1989. "The Three Waves of Modernity," in *An Introduction to Political Philosophy: Ten Essays by Leo Strauss,* Detroit: Wayne State University Press.

———. 1965. *Natural Right and History,* Chicago: University of Chicago Press.

Tessitore, Aristide. 2007. "Nietzsche or Socrates: Reflections on European Identity," in *Socrates: Reason or Unreason as the Foundation of European Identity,* Ann Ward ed., Newcastle, UK: Cambridge Scholars Publishing.

Tocqueville, Alexis de. 1990. *Democracy in America,* Henry Reeve trans., New York: Vintage Classics.

Trapp, Michael. 2007. "Introduction: the nineteenth- and twentieth-century Socrates," in *Socrates in the Nineteenth and Twentieth Centuries,* M.B. Trapp ed., Aldershot, UK: Ashgate Publishing.

Urbinati, Nadia. 2013. "John Stuart Mill, Romantics' Socrates, and the Public role of the Intellectual," in *John Stuart Mill: A British Socrates,* Houndmills, UK: Palgrave Macmillan.

Villa, Dana. 2001. *Socratic Citizenship,* Princeton: Princeton University Press.

Walsh, Sylvia. 1997. "On 'Feminine' and 'Masculine' Forms of Despair," in *Feminist Interpretations of Kierkegaard,* Celine Leon and Sylvia Walsh eds., University Park: Pennsylvania State University Press.

Ward, Ann. 2009. "The Immortality of the Soul and the Origin of the Cosmos in Plato's *Phaedo*," in *Matter and Form: From Natural Science to Political Philosophy*, Ann Ward ed., Lanham, MD: Lexington Books.

———. 2007. "Socratic Irony and Platonic Ideas? Kierkegaard's 'Critique' of Socrates in *The Concept of Irony*," in *Socrates: Reason or Unreason as the Foundation of European Identity*, Ann Ward ed., Newcastle: Cambridge Scholars Publishing.

———. 2003. "Abraham, Agnes and Socrates: Love and History in Kierkegaard's *Fear and Trembling*," in *Love and Friendship: Rethinking Politics and Affection in Modern Times*, Eduardo A. Velasquez ed., Lanham, MD: Lexington.

Westphal, Merold. 1998. "Kierkegaard and Hegel," in *The Cambridge Companion to Kierkegaard*, Alastair Hannay and Gordon D. Mariono eds., Cambridge: Cambridge University Press.

———. 1987. *Kierkegaard's Critique of Reason and Society* (Macon, GA: Mercer University Press.

Wilkins, Burleigh. 1974. *Hegel's Philosophy of History*, Ithaca: Cornell University Press.

Zuckert, Catherine H. 1996. *Postmodern Platos: Nietzsche, Heidegger, Gadamer, Strauss, Derrida*, Chicago: University of Chicago Press.

Index

Abraham: explicit challenge to Hegel with tragic hero and, 37–43; with implicit challenge to Hegel, 29–37; morality and, 30, 53n9; movement of finitude and, 31, 33, 42, 51; perfection of, 29

Agamemnon, 40, 43, 50

Alcibiades, 74, 126

Alexander the Great, 23, 24

Anaxagoras: material nature and, 18; with rational laws, 16, 18; reason and, 17–18; Socrates and, 13, 15–19, 21–22; theory of ideas or forms and, 17–18

Apollinian aspect of tragedy, 97, 99, 102

Apology of Socrates (Plato), 9, 57, 63, 71–72, 77

Aquinas, Thomas, 70

Arendt, Hannah, 9, 94

Aristophanes, 24, 25

art: body and, 93–94; modern drama and, 96; science and, 93

artists, 93, 101, 108, 109, 117

attack: on ones who command with herd morality, 110–112; on permissiveness with necessity of morality, 109–110

"Attempt at Self-Criticism" (Nietzsche), 91

Augustine (Saint), 126

Bertram, Ernst, 103n1, 121n12

Beyond Good and Evil (Nietzsche), 91–92, 105, 125–126; attack on permissiveness

and necessity of morality in, 8, 109–110; on herd morality and attack on ones who command, 110–112; with nobles as alternative to good and end of evil, 112–116; with Socrates, Dionysus and nobles in modern times, 116–121; with Socrates and science of morals, 107–109

The Birth of Tragedy (Nietzsche), 7, 105, 109, 125; art and body in, 93–94; "Attempt at Self-Criticism" in, 91; cosmos and suffering God in, 97–100; with mind and death of tragedy, 100–102; with tragedy as chorus and body, 95–97

body: art and, 93–94; sexuality and, 97, 98, 102, 105; tragedy as chorus and, 95–97

Bonaparte, Napoleon, 23, 24, 70

Branwell, George, 81

Caesar, Julius, 23, 24

Camus, Albert, 94

Catholic Christianity, 88–89

charity, 108

chorus: modern drama and, 95–96; satyr, 93, 95, 96–97, 99; tragedy as body and, 95–97

Christianity, 11, 71, 76n17, 114; Catholic, 88–89; criticism of, 91; morality and, 88; with philosophy and faith, 62; reasonableness of, 67–69; on sexuality,

135

About the Author

Ann Ward is professor of political science at Baylor University. Her research interests are ancient political philosophy, especially Herodotus, Plato and Aristotle, nineteenth-century political thought, and Canadian political theory. Her most recent book is *Contemplating Friendship in Aristotle's Ethics* (SUNY, 2016). She is also the author of *Herodotus and the Philosophy of Empire* (Baylor, 2008), and has edited *Classical Rationalism and the Politics of Europe* (Cambridge Scholars Publishing, 2017), *Socrates and Dionysus: Philosophy and Art in Dialogue* (Cambridge Scholars Publishing, 2013), *Matter and Form: From Natural Science to Political Philosophy* (Lexington, 2009), and *Socrates: Reason or Unreason as the Foundation of European Identity* (Cambridge Scholars Publishing, 2007). She has co-edited with Lee Ward *Natural Right and Political Philosophy: Essays in Honor of Catherine Zuckert and Michael Zuckert* (UNDP, 2013), and *The Ashgate Research Companion to Federalism* (Ashgate, 2009). She has published widely in scholarly journals, including *POLIS: The Journal of the Society for Greek Political Thought, Perspectives on Political Science, European Journal of Political Theory,* and *The European Legacy: Toward New Paradigms.*

www.ingramcontent.com/pod-product-compliance
Lightning Source LLC
Chambersburg PA
CBHW022323280326
41932CB00010B/1209